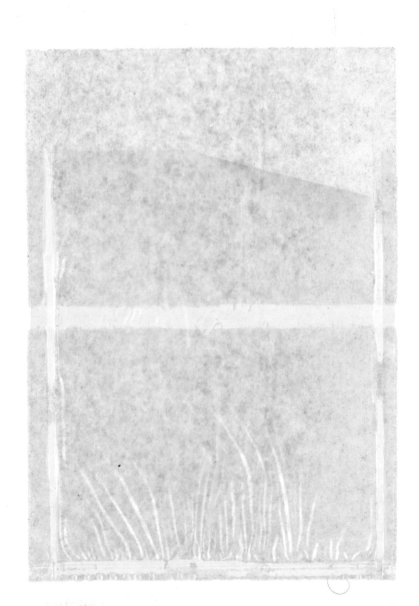

THE
BROADWAY
MUSICAL

A Complete
LP Discography

GORDON W. HODGINS

The Scarecrow Press, Inc.
Metuchen, N.J., & London 1980

Library of Congress Cataloging in Publication Data

Hodgins, Gordon W   1943-
   The Broadway musical.

   Includes indexes.
   1.   Musical revues, comedies, etc. --Discography.
I.   Title.
ML156. 4. O4H6   016. 7899'12281   80-18911
ISBN 0-8108-1343-2

★ PREFACE

For nine years I had the pleasure of selecting all records
and cassettes for the North York Public Library, Toronto,
and established and built the collections in these media in
seventeen of the Library's branches. During this time, with
the Library's collection increasing by 12, 000 items per year,
and the many requests I received for specific information
about the availability of songs and performers, it became ap-
parent that some popular areas of music did not have adequate retrospective discographies or any easy means to learn
about the contents of individual recordings. One such area
is the Broadway musical. Only what is currently available
is listed in the Schwann catalog, and usually just title, record company, and serial number are included. Library of
Congress cataloging, as found in its publication Music, Books
on Music, and Sound Recordings, does not cover all new re-
leases, and generally ignores reissues. Also, it does not
have access by title or individual songs, and only incomplete
access by performer, lyricist, and book writer. The Phono-
log catalog, while providing good detailed descriptions of individual records, is expensive and not always available.
This book through its main list and indexes provides information about all Broadway musical recordings by title, composer, performer, lyricist, book writer, and song title.
    An attempt to prepare a complete LP discography of
Broadway musicals may invite questions as to the definition

iii

of a musical and the extent of coverage.   This book includes
both original cast albums and albums released to feature specific performers or groups of performers whether or not that
person or group ever actually appeared on stage in the musical recorded.   Omitted are film soundtrack albums and
miscellaneous collections from the works of one or more composers unless the latter were presented on stage as revues.
In order to be as comprehensive as possible, works that are
on the borderline of musical comedy, such as small revues,
are included.

      The list only includes releases by the large commer-
cial North American recording companies, since the major-
ity of such records should be available in many public library collections.   Pirate editions, limited editions, and
records only available by mail order have been omitted.

      Reports of errors, suggestions for further editions,
and additional information on the musicals listed in the appendix would very much be appreciated.   I would like to
thank my wife for her patience while I was busy gathering
data for this book and for her great help with proofreading.

G. W. H.

★ CONTENTS

★ INTRODUCTION

The first section of this book lists all musicals and the albums associated with them alphabetically by title. A typical entry is as follows:

Kiss me, Kate. OC
Columbia OL 4140 (1950); Columbia OS 2300 (1963); Columbia S 32609 (1973)
Cast: Alfred Drake, Patricia Morison, Lisa Kirk.
Credits: Music and lyrics, Cole Porter; book, Bella and Samuel Spewack.
Songs: Another op'nin', another show. Why can't you behave? Wunderbar. So in love. We open in Venice. Tom, Dick or Harry. I've come to wive it wealthily in Padua. I hate men. Were thine that special face. Too darn hot. Where is the life that late I led? Always true to you. Bianca. Brush up your Shakespeare. I am ashamed that women are so simple. So kiss me, Kate.

The letters OC after the title indicate that this is an original cast album. Original cast albums that were not Broadway or off-Broadway productions have this fact stated at the end of the "Cast" line, e. g. :

Cast: Topol, Miriam Karlin; original London cast.

Similarly, original cast albums that were not the first Broadway production include further information about the performance at the end of the "Cast" line, e. g. :

Cast: Risë Stevens, Darren McGavin; original cast from the Music Theater of Lincoln Center.

1

The second line provides information about the record company, record serial number, and date of release for both the original release and subsequent reissues.   Only the main performers are listed under "Cast, " but if there is any question as to a part being main or supporting, the performer's name is included.   The "Credits" line lists the composer, lyricist, and author of the book.   If the music or book was based on another work, this information is also mentioned, e. g. :

> Credits: Music, lyrics, and book, Frank Loesser; based on Sidney Howard's They knew what they wanted.
> Credits: Musical adaptation and lyrics, Robert Wright and George Forrest; book, Milton Lazarus; based on the music of Edvard Grieg.

The "Songs" paragraph includes the songs in the order they appear on the disc.   Overtures, record bands with titles like "Opening medley" and "Finale, " and reprises are excluded. As the songs are almost always very much the same in all productions of a musical, they are only listed under one entry even though there may be two or more recordings of a particular musical.   In some places, songs for long-unavailable or quickly deleted albums have been omitted.

The main list is followed by six indexes.   The indexes for composer, lyricist, book writer, and performer are complete; however, because of the number of songs involved, the song index covers only a selection of all songs. Of the 331 different musicals in the main list, the songs for 94 are indexed completely and for 112 more are indexed partially.   While any incomplete list involves subjective decisions, every attempt has been made to include the important and memorable songs from each show indexed.   Title songs are omitted, as they can obviously be found by using the main list.   Similarly, the numerical index by record company is a partial listing, but although restricted to five primary companies, it still covers 280 of all the 424 entries in the main list.   The composer-lyricist index is a ready reference to famous names in musical comedy, e. g. , Rodgers and Hammerstein, Lerner and Loewe, and provides a complete listing of the work each pair did together that was or is available on record.

Finally, there are some records that appear to have been released but for which adequate information was not available.   These have been included in an appendix with the hope that knowledge of their existence will be useful.

★ ALPHABETICAL LIST OF BROADWAY MUSICALS

The Act. OC
DRG Records DRG 6101 (1978)
Cast: Liza Minnelli, Barry Nelson.
Credits: Music, John Kander; lyrics, Fred Ebb; book,
George Furth.
Songs: Shine it on. It's the strangest thing. Bobo's. Turn-
ing (Shaker hymn). Little do they know. Arthur in the
afternoon. The money tree. City lights. There when I
need him. Hot enough for you? My own space. Walking
papers.

✳ Ain't misbehavin' OC
RCA CBL 2-2965 (1978)
Cast: Nell Carter, Andre de Shields, Ken Page, Armelia
McQueen, Charlaine Woodward.
Credits: Music, chiefly by Fats Waller.
Songs: Ain't misbehavin' Lookin' good but feelin' bad.
'T ain't nobody's biz-ness if I do. Honeysuckle rose.
Squeeze me. Handful of keys. I've got a feeling I'm
falling. How ya baby. The jitterbug waltz. The ladies
who sing with the band. Yacht club swing. When the
nylons bloom again. Cash for your trash. Off-time.
The joint is jumpin! Spreadin' rhythm around. Lounging
at the Waldorf. The viper's drag. The reefer song.

Mean to me.   Your feet's too big.   That ain't right.
Keepin' out of mischief now.   Find out what they like.
Fat and greasy.   Black and blue.   I'm gonna sit right
down and write myself a letter.   Two sleepy people.   I've
got my fingers crossed.   I can't give you anything but
love.   It's a sin to tell a lie.

All American.   OC
Columbia KOL   5760/KOS   2160 (1962)
Cast: Ray Bolger.
Credits: Lyrics, Lee Adams; music, Charles Strouse.
Songs: Melt us.   What a country!   Our children.   We speak
the same language.   It's fun to think.   Once upon a time.
Nightlife.   I've just seen her.   Physical fitness.   The
fight song.   I couldn't have done it alone.   If I were you.
Have a dream.   I'm fascinating.   The real me.   Which
way?

Allegro.   OC
RCA Victor LOC/LSO   1099 (1965); RCA Red Seal CBM
1-2758 (1978)
Cast: John Battles, Annamary Dickey.
Credits: Music, Richard Rodgers; lyrics, Oscar Hammer-
stein II.
Songs: So far.   A fellow needs a girl.   You are never away.
The gentleman is a dope.   Joseph Taylor, Jr.   I know it
can happen again.   One foot, other foot.   To have and to
hold.   Wish them well.   Money isn't everything.   Allegro.
Coming home.

Anne of Green Gables.   OC
Columbia ELS   354 (1969)
Cast: Barbara Hamilton, Polly James, Hiram Sherman; orig-
inal London cast.
Credits: Music, Norman Campbell; lyrics, Donald Harron,
Norman Campbell (adapted from the novel by L. M. Mont-
gomery, by D. Harron)
Songs: Where is Matthew going?   Gee, I'm glad I'm no one
else but me.   We clearly requested.   The facts.   Humble
pie.   Oh Mrs. Lynde.   Back to school.   Did you hear?
Ice cream.   Where did the summer go to?   Wonderin'.
Learn everything.   Kindred spirits.   When I say my say.
I'll show him.   General store.   Anne of Green Gables.
The words.   If it hadn't been for me.

Annie.   OC
Columbia PS   34712 (1977)

Cast: Andrea McArdle, Reid Shelton, Dorothy Loudon.
Credits: Music, Charles Strouse; lyrics, Martin Charnin;
book, Thomas Meehan.
Songs: Maybe. The hard-knock life. Tomorrow. We'd
like to thank you Herbert Hoover. Little girls. I think
I'm gonna like it here. N. Y. C. Easy street. You won't
be an orphan for long. You're never fully dressed without a smile. Something was missing. I don't need
anything but you. Annie. A New Deal for Christmas.

Annie get your gun. OC
Decca DL 9018/79018 (1955); MCA Records MCA 2031
(1973)
Cast: Ethel Merman, Ray Middleton.
Credits: Music and lyrics, Irving Berlin; book, Herbert and
Dorothy Fields.
Songs: Colonel Buffalo Bill. I'm a bad, bad man. Doin'
what comes natur'lly. The girl that I marry. You can't
get a man with a gun. There's no business like show
business. They say it's wonderful. Moonshine lullaby.
My defenses are down. I'm an Indian too. I got lost in
his arms. I got the sun in the morning. An old fashioned
wedding. Anything you can do.

Annie get your gun.
Capitol W 913 (1957)
Cast: Mary Martin, John Raitt.
Credits: Music and lyrics, Irving Berlin; book, Herbert and
Dorothy Fields.

Annie get your gun.
Columbia OS 2360 (1963)
Cast: Doris Day, Robert Goulet.
Credits: Music and lyrics, Irving Berlin; book, Herbert and
Dorothy Fields.

Annie get your gun.
London XPS 905 (1973)
Cast: Ethel Merman.
Credits: Music and lyrics, Irving Berlin; book, Herbert and
Dorothy Fields.

Annie get your gun. OC
RCA Victor LOC/LSO 1124 (1966)
Cast: Ethel Merman; cast of the Music Theater of Lincoln
Center.

Credits: Music and Lyrics, Irving Berlin;   book, Herbert
and Dorothy Fields.

Anya. OC
United Artists UAL   4133 (1965)
Cast: Lillian Gish, Michael Kermoyan, Irra Petina, Con-
stance Towers.
Credits: Music and lyrics, Robert Wright and George For-
rest (based on themes of S. Rachmaninoff);   book, George
Abbott and Guy Bolton (based on Anastasia, by Marcelle
Maurette and Guy Bolton)

✳ Anyone can whistle.   OC
Columbia KOL   6080/KOS   2480 (1964);   Columbia S 32608
(1973)
Cast: Harry Guardino, Angela Lansbury, Lee Remick.
Credits: Music and lyrics, Stephen Sondheim;   book, Arthur
Laurents.
Songs: Me and my town.   Miracle song.   Simple.   Come
play wiz me.   Anyone can whistle.   A parade in town.
Everybody says don't.   I've got you to lean on.   See what
it gets you.   With so little to be sure of.

✳ Anything goes.   OC
Epic FLM 13100/FLS   15100 (1962)
Cast: Eileen Rodgers, Hal Linden, Mickey Deems.
Credits: Music and lyrics, Cole Porter;   book, Guy Bolton,
P. G. Wodehouse, Howard Lindsay, Russel Crouse (re-
vised by Guy Bolton).
Songs: Anything goes.   You're the top.   I get a kick out of
you.   All through the night.   Blow Gabriel blow.   Bon
voyage.   It's delovely.   Heaven hop.   Friendship.   Public
enemy number one.   Let's step out.   Be like the bluebird.
Take me back to Manhattan.

Anything goes.
Monmouth-Evergreen MES   7049 (1972)
Cast: Jack Whiting.
Credits: Music and lyrics, Cole Porter.
Songs: All through the night.   You're the top.

Anything goes.
Columbia ML   4751 (1954);   CSP AML   4751 (1973)
Cast: Mary Martin
Credits: Music and lyrics, Cole Porter;   book, Guy Bolton,
P. G. Wodehouse, Howard Lindsay, Russel Crouse (re-
vised by Guy Bolton).

*Applause. OC
ABC   OCS-11 (1970)
Cast: Lauren Bacall.
Credits: Music, Charles Strouse; lyrics, Lee Adams; book,
   Betty Comden and Adolph Green.
Songs: Backstage babble. Think how it's gonna be.   But
   alive. The best night of my life. Who's that girl. Ap-
   plause. Hurry back. Fasten your seat belts. Welcome
   to the theater. Good friends. She's no longer a gypsy.
   One of a kind. One hallow'een. Something greater.

The Apple tree. OC
Columbia KOL 6620/KOS 3020 (1966)
Cast: Alan Alda, Larry Blyden, Barbara Harris.
Credits: Music, Jerry Bock; lyrics, Sheldon Harnick;
   book, Bock & Harnick, based on stories by Mark Twain,
   Frank R. Stockton, Jules Feiffer.
Songs: Here in Eden. Feelings. Eve. Friends. The
   apple tree. Beautiful, beautiful world. Go to sleep,
   whatever you are. It's a fish. What makes him love
   me? I'll tell you the truth. Make way. Forbidden
   fruit. I've got what you want. Tiger, tiger. Which
   door? The lady or the tiger. Oh, to be a movie star.
   Gorgeous. Who is she? I know. Wealth. You are
   not real.

The Apple tree. OC
Trillium TR   2000 (1973)
Cast: Dinah Christie, Tom Kneebone.
Credits: Music, Jerry Bock; lyrics, Sheldon Harnick,
   book, Bock & Harnick, based on stories by Mark Twain,
   Frank R. Stockton, Jules Feiffer.

Arabian nights.
Decca DL   9013 (1954)
Credits: Music and lyrics, Carmen Lombardo and John
   Jacob Loeb; book, George Marion.

archy and mehitabel.
Columbia OL 4963 (1955); CSP AOL 4963 (1974)
Cast: Eddie Bracken, Carol Channing, David Wayne.
Credits: Music, George Kleinsinger; words, Joe Darion,
   based on the stories of Don Marquis.

At the drop of a hat. OC
Angel 35797 (1959)
Cast: Michael Flanders, Donald Swann.

Credits: Music, Donald Swann;   words, Michael Flanders.
Songs: A transport of delight.   Song of reproduction.   Green-
    sleeves.   In the bath.   A gnu.   Philological waltz.   Sat-
    ellite moon.   A happy song.   A song of the weather.   The
    reluctant cannibal.   Design for living.   Tried by the centre
    court.   Misalliance.   Madeira, m'dear?   The wom pom.
    Hippopotamus.

At the drop of another hat.   OC
Angel   36388/S36388 (1966)
Cast: Michael Flanders, Donald Swann.
Credits: Music, Donald Swann;   words, Michael Flanders.

⁂ Babes in arms.   OC
Columbia CL   823 (1956);   Columbia OL 7070/OS   2570 (1964);
    CSP AOS   2570 (1973)
Cast: Mary Martin, Mardi Bayne, Jack Cassidy.
Credits: Music, Richard Rodgers;   lyrics, Lorenz Hart;
    book, Richard Rodgers and Lorenz Hart.
Songs: Where or when.   Babes in arms.   I wish I were in
    love again.   Way out west.   My funny valentine.   Johnny
    one note.   Imagine.   All at once.   The lady is a tramp.
    You are so fair.

Bajour.   OC
Columbia KOL   6300/KOS   2700 (1964)
Cast: Herschel Bernardi, Nancy Dussault, Chita Rivera.
Credits: Music and lyrics, Walter Marks;   book, Ernest
    Kinoy.

Baker Street.   OC
MGM   7000   OC (1965)
Cast: Fritz Weaver, Inga Swenson, Martin Gabel.
Credits: Music and lyrics, Marian Grudeff and Raymond
    Jessel;   book, Jerome Coopersmith.
Songs: It's so simple.   I'm in London again.   Leave it to
    us, guy.   Letters.   Cold clear world.   Finding words
    for spring.   What a night this is going to be.   I shall
    miss you.   Roof space.   A married man.   I'd do it again.
    Pursuit.   Jewelry.

Ballad for Bimshire
London AM   48002/AMS   78002 (1963)
Credits: Music and lyrics, Irving Burgie.

The Bandwagon
Columbia ML 4751 (1954); CSP AML 4751 (1973)
Cast: Mary Martin.
Credits: Music, Arthur Schwartz; lyrics, Howard Dietz;
book, Howard Dietz and George S. Kaufman.
Songs: It better be good. Hoops. High and low. Confes-
sion. New sun in the sky. Dancing in the dark. I love
Louisa. Where can he be?

The Believers. OC
RCA Victor LOC/LSO 1151 (1968)
Cast: Voices Incorporated.
Credits: Music and lyrics, Voices Incorporated.

Bells are ringing. OC
Columbia OL 5170/OS 2006 (1958)
Cast: Judy Holliday, Sydney Chaplin.
Credits: Music, Jule Styne; book and lyrics, Betty Comden
and Adolph Green.
Songs: Bells are ringing. It's a perfect relationship. On
my own. It's a simple little system. Is it a crime?
Hello, hello there! I met a girl. Long before I knew
you. Mu-cha-cha. Just in time. Drop that name. The
party's over. Salzburg. The Midas touch. I'm goin'
back.

Ben Franklin in Paris. OC
Capitol VAS/SVAS 2191 (1964)
Cast: Robert Preston.
Credits: Music, Mark Sandrich; lyrics, Sidney Michaels.

Beowulf
Daffodil DAFF 10050 (1974)
Cast: Holiday Festival Singers.
Credits: Music, Victor Davies; libretto and lyrics, Betty
Jane Wylie.
Songs: I sing the song of the beginning. Death is not easy
to hide from.

Berlin to Broadway with Kurt Weill. OC
Paramount PAS 4000 (1973)
Cast: Margery Cohen, Ken Kercheval, Judy Lander, Jerry
Lanning, Hal Watters.
Credits: Music, Kurt Weill; text and format, Gene Lerner.
Songs: How to survive. Barbara song. Useless song.
Jealousy duet. Mack the knife. March ahead to the fight.
Don't be afraid. Bilbao song. Surabaya Johnny. Child-

hood's bright endeavour.   Mandalay song.   Alabama song.
Deep in Alaska.   Oh heavenly salvation.   As you make
your bed.   Pirate Jenny.   I wait for a ship.   Sailor tango.
Johnny Johnson.   Songs of peace and war.   A hymn to
peace.   Listen to my song.   How can you tell an Ameri-
can.   September song.   Girl of the moment.   Saga of
Jenny.   My ship.   Speak low.   That's him.   Progress.
Ain't it awful, the heat.   Lonely house.   Trouble man.
Train to Johannesburg.   Cry, the beloved country.   Lost
in the stars.   Love life.

Best foot forward
Stet Records DS   15003   (1977)
Cast: Liza Minnelli, Paula Wayne.
Credits: Music, Hugh Martin;   lyrics, Ralph Blane;   book,
John Cecil Holm.
Songs: Wish I may.   Three men on a date.   Hollywood
story.   The three "B's."   Ev'ry time.   Alive and kicking.
The guy who brought me.   Shady lady bird.   Buckle down
Winsocki.   You're lucky.   What do you think I am?   A
raving beauty.   Just a little joint with a juke box.   You
are for loving.

Beyond the fringe.   OC
Capitol W/SW   1792   (1962)
Cast: Alan Bennett, Peter Cook, Jonathan Miller, Dudley
Moore.
Credits: Music, Dudley Moore.
Songs: Bollard.   The sadder and wiser beaver.   Deutscher.
Chansons.   Take a pew.   Aftermyth of the war.   Sitting
on the bench.   And the same to you Colonel Bogey.
Portrait from memory.   So that's the way you like it.
The end of the world.

Beyond the fringe '64.   OC
Capitol W/SW   2072   (1964);   Capitol ST 11654   (1977)
Cast: Alan Bennett, Peter Cook, Dudley Moore, Paxton
Whitehead.
Credits: Music, Dudley Moore.
Songs: Home thoughts from abroad.   The English way of
death.   Royal box.   One leg too few.   Lord Cobbold/The
Duke.   Real class.   A piece of my mind.   The great
train robbery.

Big Man.
Fantasy F 79006   (1975)
Cast: Randy Crawford, Robert Guillaume, Joe Williams.

Credits: Music, Julian and Nat Adderley; lyrics, Diane
Lampert and Peter Farrow; book, Diane Lampert and
George W. George, from material by Paul Avila Mayer,
G. W. George, and Peter Farrow.
Songs: Anybody need a big man? Forty more miles to go.
Ten mile of mountain. Gonna give lovin' a try. The
broomstick song. Next year in Jerusalem. Stayin' place.
A new star risin'. Grind your own coffee. Hundred an'
one year. Born black. Poundin'. Jesus where you now?
If I was Jehovah. On his bones.

Bitter sweet.
Odeon Studio 2 TWO 273 (1968)
Cast: June Bronhill, Neville Jason, Julia D'Alba, Leslie
Fyson.
Credits: Music, book, and lyrics, Noël Coward.
Songs: The call of life. If you could only come with me.
I'll see you again. What is love. Ladies of the town.
If love were all. Dear little cafe. Tokay. Kiss me.
Green carnations. Zigeuner.

Bitter sweet.
Angel 35814 (1960)
Cast: Robert Cardinall, Vanessa Lee.
Credits: Music, book, and lyrics, Noël Coward.

Black nativity. OC
Trip TLP 7022 (1975)
Cast: Marion Williams, Princess Stewart, Alex Bradford.
Songs: My way's cloudy. Most done traveling. Baby born
today. Poor little Jesus boy. Mary, what you gonna
name that pretty little baby? Wasn't that a mighty day?
Joy to the world. Christ is born. Rise up shepherd
and follow. Sweet little Jesus boy. Oh come all ye
faithful. If anybody ask you who. Go where I send thee.

Blackbirds of 1928.
Columbia OL 6770 (1968)
Cast: Cab Calloway, Duke Ellington, Adelaide Hall, Ethel
Waters.
Credits: Music, James McHugh; lyrics, Dorothy Fields.
Songs: I can't give you anything but love. Doin' the new
low down. I must have that man. Baby! Diga diga do.
Shuffle your feet (and just roll along). Porgy. St. Louis
blues. Exploitation record.

Bloomer girl. OC
Decca 8015 (1954); Decca 9126/79126 (1966); MCA Records

MCA-2072 (1973)
Cast: Celeste Holm.
Credits: Music, Harold Arlen;   lyrics, E. Y. Harburg;
   book, Sid Herzig and Fred Saidy.
Songs: When the boys come home.   Evelina.   Welcome
   hinges.   The farmer's daughter.   It was good enough
   for grandma.   The eagle and me.   Right as the rain.
   T'morra' t'morra.   The rakish young man with the
   whiskahs.   Sunday in Cicero Falls.   I got a song.   Satin
   gown and silver shoe.   Liza crossing the ice.   Never
   was born.   Man for sale.

The Boy friend.   OC
RCA Victor   LOC   1018 (1954)
Cast: Julie Andrews, Ruth Altman, Ann Wakefield.
Credits: Book, music, and lyrics, Sandy Wilson.
Songs: Perfect young ladies.   The boy friend.   Fancy for-
   getting.   Won't you Charleston with me?   I could be happy
   with you.   Sur la plage.   A room in Bloomsbury.   The
   you don't want to play with me blues.   Safety in numbers.
   The Riviera.   It's never too late to fall in love.   Car-
   nival tango.   Poor little Pierrette.

The Boy friend.
Decca   DL   79177 (1970);   MCA Records   MCA   2074 (1973)
Cast: Judy Carne, Sandy Duncan.
Credits: Book, music, and lyrics, Sandy Wilson.

The Boys from Syracuse.
Columbia   ML   4837 (1954);   Columbia   CL   847 (1956);
   Columbia   OL   7080/OS   2580 (1964);   CSP COS   2580
   (1973)
Cast: Jack Cassidy, Portia Nelson, Bibi Osterwald.
Credits: Music, Richard Rodgers; lyrics, Lorenz Hart; book,
   George Abbott.
Songs: He had twins.   Dear old Syracuse.   What can you
   do with a man.   Falling in love with love.   The shortest
   day of the year.   This can't be love.   Ladies of the even-
   ing.   He and she.   You have cast your shadow on the sea.
   Come with me.   Sing for your supper.   Oh, Diogenes.

Bravo Giovanni.   OC
Columbia KOL 5800/KOS   2200 (1962)
Cast: Michele Lee, David Opatoshu, Cesare Siepi.
Credits: Music, Milton Schafer;   lyrics, Ronny Graham.

Brigadoon.
Columbia CL 1132 (1958);   Columbia OL 7040/OS   2540 (1964);

CSP COS   2540 (1973)
Cast: Jack Cassidy, Shirley Jones.
Credits: Music, Frederick Loewe;   book and lyrics, Alan
   Jay Lerner.
Songs: Brigadoon.   Vendors' calls.   Down on MacConnachy
   Square.   Waitin' for my dearie.   I'll go home with Bonnie
   Jean.   The heather on the hill.   The love of my life.
   Jeannie's packin' up.   Come to me, bend to me.   Almost
   like being in love.   The chase.   There but for you go I.
   My mother's wedding day.   From this day on.

Brigadoon.   OC
RCA Victor LSO   1001 (1963);   RCA Victor LOC   1001 (1966)
Cast: Cast of Cheryl Crawford's production.
Credits: Music, Frederick Loewe;   book and lyrics, Alan
   Jay Lerner.

Bubbling brown sugar.   OC
H&L Records HL   69011-698 (1967)
Cast: Avon Long, Josephine Premice, Vivian Reed, Joseph
   Attles.
Credits: Book, Loften Mitchell.
Songs: Bubbling brown sugar.   Nobody.   His eye is on the
   sparrow.   Swing low, sweet chariot.   Sophisticated lady.
   Stormy Monday blues.   In honeysuckle time, when Emaline
   said she'd be mine.   Sweet Georgia Brown.   Honeysuckle
   Rose.   I got it bad.   Harlem makes me feel!   There'll
   be some changes made.   God bless the child.   It don't
   mean a thing.

By Jupiter.   OC
RCA Victor LOC/LSO   1137 (1967)
Cast: Bob Dishy.
Credits: Music, Richard Rodgers;   lyrics, Lorenz Hart;
   book, Richard Rodgers, Lorenz Hart.

By the beautiful sea.   OC
Capitol S   531 (1954);   Capitol T   11652 (1977)
Cast: Shirley Booth, Wilbur Evans.
Credits: Music, Arthur Schwartz;   lyrics, Dorothy Fields;
   book, Herbert and Dorothy Fields.
Songs: The sea song.   Old enough to love.   Coney Island
   boat.   Alone too long.   Happy habit.   Good time Charlie.
   I'd rather wake up by myself.   Hooray for George the
   Third.   Hang up!   More love than your love.   Lottie Gib-
   son specialty.   Throw the anchor away.

Bye bye Birdie.   OC
Columbia KOL 5510/KOS   2025 (1960);   CSP COS   2025 (1973)
Cast: Chita Rivera, Dick Van Dyke.
Credits: Music, Charles Strouse;   lyrics, Lee Adams;
   book, Michael Stewart.
Songs: An English teacher.   The telephone hour.   How
   lovely to be a woman.   Put on a happy face.   Normal
   American boy.   One boy.   Honestly sincere.   Hymn for
   a Sunday evening.   One last kiss.   What did I ever see
   in him?   A lot of livin' to do.   Kids.   Baby, talk to me.
   Spanish Rose.   Rosie.

* Cabaret.   OC
Columbia KOL 6640/KOS   3040 (1966)
Cast: Bert Convy, Jack Gilford, Joel Grey, Jill Haworth,
   Lotte Lenya.
Credits: Music, John Kander;   lyrics, Fred Ebb;   book,
   Joe Masteroff.
Songs: Willkommen.   So what?   Don't tell mama.   Tele-
   phone song.   Perfectly marvellous.   Two ladies.   It couldn't
   please me more.   Tomorrow belongs to me.   Why should I
   wake up?   The money song.   Married.   Meeskite.   If you
   could see her.   What would you do?   Cabaret.

Cabin in the sky.   OC
Capitol W/SW   2073 (1964)
Credits: Music, Vernon Duke;   lyrics, John Latouche;
   book, Lynn Root.
Songs: Happiness is just a thing called Joe.   Life's full
   of consequences.   Li'l black sheep.   Ain't it the truth.
   Cabin in the sky.   Taking a chance on love.   Honey in
   the honeycomb.   In my old Virginia home.   Going up.
   Things ain't what they used to be.

Call me madam.
Decca 9022 (1955);   MCA Records MCA   2055 (1971)
Cast: Ethel Merman.
Credits: Music and lyrics, Irving Berlin;   book, Howard
   Lindsay and Russel Crouse.
Songs: The hostess with the mostes' on the ball.   Washington Square dance.   Lichtenburg.   Can you use any money
   today?   Marrying for love.   The ocarina.   It's a lovely
   day today.   The best thing for you.   Something to dance
   about.   Once upon a time today.   They like Ike.   You're
   just in love.

Call me madam. OC
Monmouth Evergreen MES   7073 (1975)
Cast: Billie Worth, Anton Walbrook, Jeff Warren; original
London cast.
Credits: Music and lyrics, Irving Berlin; book, Howard
Lindsay and Russel Crouse.

Call me madam. OC
RCA CBM   1-2032 (1976)
Cast: Dinah Shore.
Credits: Music and lyrics, Irving Berlin; book, Howard
Lindsay and Russel Crouse.

Camelot. OC
Columbia KOL 5620/KOS   2031 (1961);   Columbia OL 5620/OS
2031 (1967);   Columbia S 32602 (1973)
Cast: Julie Andrews, Richard Burton, Robert Goulet.
Credits: Music, Frederick Loewe; book and lyrics, Alan
Jay Lerner.
Songs: I wonder what the King is doing tonight.   The simple
joys of maidenhood.   Camelot.   Follow me.   The lusty
month of May.   C'est moi.   Then you may take me to
the fair.   How to handle a woman.   If ever I would leave
you.   Parade.   Before I gaze at you again.   The seven
deadly virtues.   What do the simple folk do?   Fie on
goodness.   I loved you once in silence.   Guenevere.

Can-can. OC
Capitol S-452 (1953);   Capitol DW   452 (1969)
Cast: Gwen Verdon, Hans Conried.
Credits: Music and lyrics, Cole Porter; book, Abe Burrows.
Songs: Can can.   It's alright with me.   Come along with
me.   Live and let live.   You do something to me.   Let's
do it.   Montmartre.   C'est magnifique. Maidens typical of
France.   Snake dance.   Just one of those things.   I love
Paris.   I am in love.

Can-can. OC
Monmouth Evergreen MES   7073 (1975)
Cast: Irene Hilda, Edmund Hockridge; original London cast.
Credits: Music and lyrics, Cole Porter; book, Abe Burrows.

Candide. OC
Columbia S2X/Q2S   32923 (1974)
Cast: Mark Baker, Maureen Brennan, Lewis J. Stadlen.
Credits: Music, Leonard Bernstein; lyrics, Richard Wilbur,
John Latouche, and Dorothy Parker; book, Lillian Hellman.

Songs: Life is happiness indeed. Parade. The best of all possible worlds. Oh happy we. It must be so. O miserere. Glitter and be gay. Auto da fe. This world. You were dead, you know. The rich jew and the grand inquisitor. I am easily assimilated. My love. Alleluia. Sheep's song. Bon voyage. Make our garden grow.

Candide.
Columbia OL 5180/OS 2350 (1963)
Cast: Max Adrian, Robert Rounseville.
Credits: Music, Leonard Bernstein; lyrics, Richard Wilbur, John Latouche, and Dorothy Parker; book, Lillian Hellman.

Cantata Canada.
Century II SPAL 17000 (1973)
Cast: Privilege.
Credits: Orchestrations, Gerry Derre and Al McGee.
Songs: In the dawning. Beware of the heavyhand. The companies. The plains of Abraham. A hit or a miss. Klondike. The great depression farmer's lament. Bookends for a nation. The hired man. Northlands destiny. Strangers from a strange land.

Canterbury tales.   OC
Capitol SW 229 (1969)
Cast: Hermione Baddeley, Martyn Green, George Rose.
Credits: Music, Richard V. Hill and John Hawkins; lyrics, Nevill Coghill; book, Martin Starkie and Nevill Coghill.
Songs: Song of welcome. Goodnight hymn. Canterbury day. I have a noble cock. Darling, let me teach you how to kiss. There's the moon. It depends on what you're at. Love will conquer all. Beer is best mug dance. Come on and marry me, honey. Where are the girls of yesterday. Hymen, hymen. If she has never loved before. I'll give my love a ring. Pear tree quintet. I am all ablaze. What do women want? April song.

Carmen Jones.   OC
Decca 9021 (1955); MCA Records MCA-2054 (1971)
Cast: Muriel Smith, Luther Saron.
Credits: Music, Georges Bizet; book and lyrics, Oscar Hammerstein II.
Songs: Dat's love. Dere's a cafe on de corner. Beat dat rhythm on a drum. Stan' up and fight. Whizzin' away along de track. Dis flower. My Joe. Dat's our man.

Carmilla. OC
Vanguard VSD 79322 (1972)
Credits: Music, Ben Johnston.
Songs: Our household. A dream. By moonlight. On the
idyllic influence of the moon. An invitation. Carmilla
stays. We compare notes. A saunter. Twilight. A
funeral passes by. A mountebank. The amulet. A
strange agony. Passing days. Descending. Mesmerized.

Carnival! OC
MGM E/SE 3946 OC (1961)
Cast: Anna Maria Alberghetti, James Mitchell, Kaye
Ballard.
Credits: Music and lyrics, Bob Merrill; book, Michael
Stewart.
Songs: Direct from Vienna. Mira. The sword, the rose
and the cape. Very nice man. I've got to find a man.
Yes, my heart. Humming. Grand imperial cirque de
Paris. Her face. Yum, ticky, ticky, tum, tum. The
rich. Everybody likes you. I hate him. It was always
you. She's my love.

⨉ Carousel. OC
Decca DL 9020 (1957); Decca DL 79020 (1967); MCA
Records MCA-2033 (1973)
Cast: John Raitt, Jan Clayton.
Credits: Music, Richard Rodgers; book and lyrics, Oscar
Hammerstein II.
Songs: You're a queer one, Julie Jordan. Mister Snow.
If I loved you. June is bustin' out all over. When the
children are asleep. Blow high, blow low. This was a
real nice clambake. There's nothin' so bad for a woman.
What's the use of wond'rin'. The highest judge of all.
You'll never walk alone.

Carousel.
Command RS 33-843 (1962)
Cast: Alfred Drake, Roberta Peters.
Credits: Music, Richard Rodgers; book and lyrics, Oscar
Hammerstein II.

Carousel. OC
RCA Victor LOC/LSO 1114 (1965)
Cast: Eileen Christy, John Raitt; original cast of the
Music Theater of Lincoln Center.
Credits: Music, Richard Rodgers; book and lyrics, Oscar
Hammerstein II.

Carousel.
RCA Victor LPM   1048 (1955)
Cast: Robert Merrill, Patrice Munsel.
Credits: Music, Richard Rodgers; book and lyrics, Oscar
  Hammerstein II.

The Carpenter's son.
RCA Victor CPL   20-0419 (1973)
Cast: Orsa Lia, Ray Walker, Jack Eric Williams, Alex
  Zanetis, Jordanaires.
Credits: Music, lyrics, and book, Alex Zanetis.

Celebration. OC
Capitol SW   198 (1969)
Cast: Ted Thurston, Susan Watson.
Credits: Music, Harvey Schmidt; words, Tom Jones.

Chicago. OC
Arista AL   9005 (1975)
Cast: Gwen Verdon, Chita Rivera, Jerry Orbach.
Credits: Music, John Kander; book, Fred Ebb and Bob
  Fosse; lyrics, Fred Ebb.
Songs: All that jazz. Funny honey. Cell block tango.
  When you're good to mama. All I care about. A little
  bit of good. We both reached for the gun. Roxie. I
  can't do it alone. My own best friend. Me and my
  baby. Mr. Cellophane. When Velma takes the stand.
  Razzle dazzle. Class. Nowadays.

A Chorus line. OC
Columbia PS   33581 (1975)
Cast: Original cast of the New York Shakespeare Festival
  production.
Credits: Music, Marvin Hamlisch; lyrics, Edward Kleban;
  book, James Kirkwood and Nicholas Dante.
Songs: I hope I get it. I can do that. At the ballet. Sing!
  Hello twelve, hello thirteen, hello love. Nothing. The
  music and the mirror. Dance: ten; looks: three. One.
  What I did for love.

Christine. OC
Columbia OL 5520/OS   2026 (1960)
Cast: Maureen O'Hara.
Credits: Music, Sammy Fain.

Cinderella.
Columbia OL   5190 (1957); Columbia OS   2005 (1958)
Cast: Edith Adams, Julie Andrews, Howard Lindsey, Dorothy

Stickney.
Credits: Music, Richard Rodgers; book and lyrics, Oscar
Hammerstein II.
Songs: In my own little corner. The prince is giving a
ball. Impossible! Ten minutes ago. Stepsisters' lament.
Do I love you because you're beautiful? A lovely night.

Cinderella.
Columbia OL 6330/OS 2730 (1965)
Cast: Pat Carroll, Stuart Damon, Don Heitgerd, Celeste
Holm, Walter Pidgeon, Ginger Rogers, Barbara Ruick,
Jo Van Fleet, Lesley Ann Warren.
Credits: Music, Richard Rodgers; book and lyrics, Oscar
Hammerstein II.

Coco.
Paramount PMS 1002 (1970)
Cast: Katharine Hepburn.
Credits: Music, André Previn; book and lyrics, Alan J.
Lerner.
Songs: That's the way you are. The world belongs to the
young. Let's go home. Mademoiselle Cliche de Paris.
On the corner of the Rue Cambon. The money rings out
like freedom. A brand new dress. A woman is how she
loves. Gabrielle. Coco. When your lover says goodbye.
Fiasco. Orbach's, Bloomingdale's, Best & Sak's. Always
mademoiselle.

Cole. OC
RCA Red Seal CRL 2 5054 (1974)
Credits: Music and lyrics, Cole Porter; devised by Benny
Green and Alan Strachan.
Songs: Night and day. Wouldn't it be fun. Another op'nin',
another show. The bobolink waltz. Bingo Eli Yale.
Gerald Murphy remembers. When the summer moon
comes 'long. Leaving Yale. See America first. Leaving
home. The lost liberty blues. Paris in the '20's. I
love Paris. Playboy. Not all play. Dizzy baby. Going
home. You don't know Paree. Take me back to Manhattan. I happen to like New York. I'm a gigolo. News
extra! Love for sale. Down in the depths. A new white
way. Anything goes. I get a kick out of you. No sorrow
tomorrow. Begin the beguine. What is this thing called
love. You do something to me. You've got to have that
thing. Let's misbehave. The laziest gal in town. At
long last love. It's de-lovely. In the still of the night.
I worship you. Make it another old-fashioned, please.

Most gentlemen don't like love.   From this moment on.
Just one of those things.   We shall never be younger.
Go west.   Be a clown.   Looking east.   Please don't mon-
key with Broadway.   The leader of a big-time band.   Dol-
drums.   Brush up your Shakespeare.   Why can't you behave?   Last words.   Ev'ry time we say goodbye.   Tomorrow.

Company.   OC
Columbia OS   3550 (1970)
Cast: Dean Jones, Elaine Stritch, Barbara Barrie.
Credits: Music and lyrics, Stephen Sondheim;   book, George
Furth.
Songs: The little things you do together.   Sorry-grateful.
You could drive a person crazy.   Have I got a girl for
you.   Someone is waiting.   Another hundred people.
Getting married today.   Side by side by side.   What
would we do without you.   Poor baby.   Tick-tock.   Bar-
celona.   The ladies who lunch.   Being alive.

Conversation piece.
CSP ASL   163 (1970?)
Cast: Lily Pons, Noël Coward.
Credits: Music, book, and lyrics, Noël Coward.
Songs: I'll follow my secret heart.   Regency rakes.   Charm-
ing, charming, charming.   Dear little soldiers.   There's
always something fishy about the French.   English lesson.
There was once a little village.   Nevermore.

Cowardy custard.   OC
RCA Victor LSO   6010 (1973)
Cast: Original cast of the Mermaid Theatre's City of London festival production.
Credits: Music and lyrics, Noël Coward;   devised by Gerald Frow, Alan Strachan, and Wendy Toye.
Songs: If love were all.   I'll see you again.   Time and
again.   Has anybody seen our ship?   Try to learn to
love.   Kiss me.   Go slow, Johnny.   Tokay.   Dearest
love.   Could you please oblige us with a bren gun?   Come
the wild, wild weather.   Spinning song.   Parisian Pierrot.
You were there.   Any little fish.   A room with a view.
New York poverty.   When you want me.   Specially for
you.   Beatnik love affair.   Success.   I'm mad about you.
Poor little rich girl.   Louisa.   Mad about the boy.   The
stately homes of England.   Twentieth Century blues.   I
went to a marvellous party.   Auditions.   Mrs. Worthington.
Why must the show go on?   London pride.   London is a

little bit of all right.   What ho, Mrs. Brisket.   Don't
take our Charlie for the army.   Saturday night at the
Rose and Crown.   London at night.   There are bad times
just around the corner.   Alice is at it again.   I love
travelling.   The passenger's always right.   Useful phrases.
Why do the wrong people travel?   St. Peter's.   Mad dogs
and Englishmen.   Nina, I like America.   Bronxville Darby
and Joan.   Darjeeling.   I wonder what happened to him?
Miss Mouse.   Let's do it.   Last words.   Touring days.
Nothing can last forever.   Would you like to stick a pin
in my balloon?   Mary make-believe.   Dance, little lady.
Men about town.   Forbidden fruit.   Sigh no more.   Younger generation.   I'll follow my secret heart.

Cricket on the hearth.
RCA LOC/LSO   1140 (1967)
Cast: Danny Thomas.
Credits: Music, Maury Laws;   lyrics, Jules Bass.

Cyrano.
A & M SP   3702 (1973)
Cast: Christopher Plummer.
Credits: Music, Michael J. Lewis;   lyrics, Anthony Bur-
    gess;   book based on Anthony Burgess' adaption of Cyrano
    de Bergerac, by Edmond Rostand.
Songs: Nose song.   Tell her.   From now till forever.   Ber-
    gerac.   No thank you.   Roxana.   It's she and it's me.   You
    have made me love.   Thither, thother, thide of the ...
    Pocapdedious.   Paris cuisine.   Love is not love.   Autumn
    carol.   I never loved you.

Dames at sea.   OC
Columbia OS   3330 (1969)
Cast: David Christmas, Bernadette Peters, Tamara Long,
    Joseph R. Sicari.
Credits: Music, Jim Wise;   book and lyrics, George Haim-
    sohn and Robin Miller.
Songs: Wall Street.   It's you.   Broadway baby.   That mister
    man of mine.   Choo-choo honeymoon.   The sailor of my
    dreams.   Good times are here to stay.   Dames at sea.
    The beguine.   Raining in my heart.   Singapore Sue.
    There's something about you.   The echo waltz.   Star tar.
    Let's have a simple wedding.

Damn Yankees.   OC
RCA Victor LOC   1021 (1955);   RCA Victor LSO 1021 (1968)
Cast: Stephen Douglass, Gwen Verdon, Ray Walston.
Credits: Music and lyrics, Jerry Ross and Richard Adler;
    book, George Abbott and Douglass Wallop.
Songs: Six months out of every year.   Goodbye, old girl.
    Heart.   Shoeless Joe from Hannibal, Mo.   A little brains,
    a little talent.   A man doesn't know.   Whatever Lola
    wants.   Who's got the pain?   The game.   Near to you.
    Those were the good old days.   Two lost souls.

Darling of the day.   OC
RCA Victor LSO   1149 (1968)
Cast: Vincent Price, Patricia Routledge.
Credits: Music, Jule Styne;   lyrics, E. Y. Harburg;   based
    on Arnold Bennett's Buried Alive.

⁕ Dear world.   OC
Columbia BOS   3260 (1969)
Cast: Angela Lansbury, Jane Connell, Carmen Mathews.
Credits: Music and lyrics, Jerry Herman;   book, Jerome
    Lawrence and Robert E. Lee;   based on The madwoman
    of Chaillot, by Jean Giraudoux.
Songs: The spring of next year.   Each tomorrow morning.
    I don't want to know.   I've never said I love you.   Gar-
    bage.   Dear world.   Kiss her now.   The tea party.   And
    I was beautiful.   One person.

⁕ The Decline and fall of the entire world as seen through the
    eyes of Cole Porter.
Columbia OL 6410/OS   2810 (1965);   CSP AOS   2810 (1973)
Cast: Kaye Ballard, Harold Lang, Carmen Alvarez, William
    Hickey, Elmarie Wendel.
Credits: Music and lyrics, Cole Porter.
Songs: I introduced.   I'm a gigolo.   The leader of the big-
    time band.   I loved him.   I happen to like New York.
    What shall I do?   Tomorrow.   Farming.   Give him the
    oo-la-la.   Make it another old fashioned please.   Down
    in the depths.   Most gentlemen don't like love.

The Desert song.
Columbia ML   4636 (1953);   Columbia CL   831 (1956)
Cast: Nelson Eddy, Doretta Morrow, David Atkinson.
Credits: Music, Sigmund Romberg;   book and lyrics, Otto
    Harbach, Oscar Hammerstein II, and Frank Mandel.
Songs: The riff song.   Margot.   French military marching
    song.   Romance.   Then you will know.   I want a kiss.

The desert song.   Eastern and western love.   Let love
go.   One flower in your garden.   One alone.   The sabre
song.

The Desert song.
RCA Victor LM/LSC   2440 (1960)
Cast: Mario Lanza, Judith Raskin.
Credits: Music, Sigmund Romberg;   book and lyrics, Otto
   Harbach, Oscar Hammerstein II, and Frank Mandel.
Songs: The desert song.   French military song.   The riff
   song.   I want a kiss.   Let love go.   One flower in your
   garden.   Azuri's dance.   Then you will know.   Romance.
   One good boy gone wrong.   One alone.

The Desert song.
Angel   35905/S35905 (1961)
Cast: June Bronhill, Edmund Hockridge.
Credits: Music, Sigmund Romberg;   book and lyrics, Otto
   Harbach, Oscar Hammerstein II, and Frank Mandel.

The Desert song.
Capitol   T-351 (1958)
Cast: Gordon MacRae, Lucille Norman, Robert Sands, Thurl
   Ravenscroft.
Credits: Music, Sigmund Romberg;   book and lyrics, Otto
   Harbach, Oscar Hammerstein II, and Frank Mandel.

The Desert song.
Capitol W/SW   1842 (1962);   Angel S   37319 (1978)
Cast: Dorothy Kirsten, Gordon MacRae.
Credits: Music, Sigmund Romberg;   book and lyrics, Otto
   Harbach, Oscar Hammerstein II, and Frank Mandel.

The Desert song.
Monmouth Evergreen MES   7054 (1973)
Cast: Edith Day, Harry Welchman.
Credits: Music, Sigmund Romberg;   book and lyrics, Otto
   Harbach, Oscar Hammerstein II, and Frank Mandel.

The Desert song.
RCA Victor LOP/LSO   1000 (1958)
Cast: Cathy Barr, Giorgio Tozzi.
Credits: Music, Sigmund Romberg;   book and lyrics, Otto
   Harbach, Oscar Hammerstein II, and Frank Mandel.

Destry rides again.   OC
Decca DL   9075/79075 (1960)

Cast: Dolores Gray, Andy Griffith.
Credits: Music and lyrics, Harold Rome.
Songs: Ladies.   Anyone would love you.   I know your kind.
Once knew a fella.   Fair warning.   That ring on the fin-
ger.   I say hello.

Dime a dozen
Cadence CLP 3063 (1963)
Cast: Julius Monk's Plaza-9.

DisinHAIRited.
RCA Victor LSO 1163 (1970)
Cast: Jim Rado, Jerry Ragni.
Credits: Music, Galt McDermott;   lyrics, Jim Rado and
Jerry Ragni.
Songs: One thousand-year-old man.   So sing the children
on the avenue.   Manhattan beggar.   Sheila Franklin.
Reading the writing.   Washing the world.   Exanaplanatooch.
Hello there.   Mr. Berger.   I'm hung.   Climax.   Electric
blues.   I dig.   Going down.   You are standing on my bed.
The bed.   Mess o' dirt.   Dead end.   Oh great god of
power.   Eyes look your last.   Sentimental ending.

Do I hear a waltz?   OC
Columbia KOL 6370/KOS 2770 (1965);   CSP AKOS 2770
(1973)
Cast: Elizabeth Allen, Sergio Franchi.
Credits: Music, Richard Rodgers;   lyrics, Stephen Sondheim;
book, Arthur Laurents.
Songs: Someone woke up.   This week Americans.   What do
we do?   We fly.   Someone like you.   Bargaining.   Think-
ing.   No understand.   Take the moment.   Here we are
again.   Moon in my window.   We're gonna be all right.
Do I hear a waltz?   Stay.   Perfectly lovely couple.
Thank you so much.

Do-re-mi.   OC
RCA Victor LOCD/LSOD 2002 (1961);   RCA Victor LOC/LSO
1105 (1965)
Cast: Phil Silvers.
Credits: Music, Jule Styne;   lyrics, Betty Comden and Adolph
Green;   book, Garson Kanin.

Donnybrook!   OC
Kapp KDL 8500 (1961)
Cast: Eddie Foy, Jr. , Art Lund.
Credits: Music and lyrics, Johnny Burke.

Don't bother me, I can't cope. OC
Polydor PD 6013 (1972)
Cast: Alex Bradford, Micki Grant.
Credits: Music and lyrics, Micki Grant.
Songs: I gotta keep movin! Harlem streets. Lookin' over
  from your side. Don't bother me, I can't cope. Fighting
  for Pharoah. Good vibrations. You think I got rhythm?
  They keep coming. My name is man. Love power.
  Questions. Time brings about a change. So little time.
  Thank heaven for you. All I need.

Don't play us cheap. OC
Stax STS 2 3006 (1972)
Credits: Music, Melvin Van Peebles.

Dressed to the nines. OC
MGM Records E/ES 3914 OC (1961)

Dude.
Kilmarnock KIL 72003 (1972)
Cast: Salome Bey.
Credits: Music, Galt MacDermott; lyrics, Gerome Ragni.
Songs: Know your name. A garden for two. Boo boo.
  No one. I never knew. Say what you want to say.
  Happy song. Only a few more years. Jazz bridge.
  Sweet dreams blossom. Baby breath. At home.

The Elephant calf. OC
Asch FL 9831 (1968)
Cast: Hilda Brawner, Beeson Carroll, Logan Ramsey,
  Frank Groseclose.
Credits: Music, Arnold Black; book and lyrics, Bertolt
  Brecht.

Elsa Lanchester herself.
Verve V 15024 (1961)
Cast: Elsa Lanchester
Credits: Music and lyrics, Elsa Lanchester.

Ernest in love. OC
Columbia OL 5530/OS 2027 (1960)
Credits: Music, Lee Pockriss.

An Evening with Groucho.
A & M Records SP 3515 (1972)

Cast: Groucho Marx.
Songs: Hello, I must be going. Timbuctoo. Oh, how that
woman could cook. Toronto song. Always. Stay down
where you belong. Everybody works but father. Show
me a rose. Lydia, the tattooed lady.

Evergreen.
Monmouth Evergreen MES   7049 (1972)
Cast: Jessie Matthews.
Credits: Music, Richard Rodgers; lyrics, Lorenz Hart.
Songs: In the cool of the evening. If I give in to you.
Dancing on the ceiling. Dear! Dear! Tinkle. Over my
shoulder. No place but home. Just by your example.
When you've got a little springtime in your heart.

⁑Fade out, fade in. OC
ABC-Paramount ABC/ABCS   OC   3 (1964)
Cast: Carol Burnett.
Credits: Music, Jule Styne; book and lyrics, Betty Comden
and Adolph Green.

Fanny. OC
RCA Victor LOC   1015 (1954)
Cast: Ezio Pinza, Walter Slezak.
Credits: Music and lyrics, Harold Rome; book, S. N. Behr-
man and Joshua Logan; based on the trilogy by Marcel
Pagnol.
Songs: Never too late for love. Cold cream jar song. Oc-
topus song. Restless heart. Why be afraid to dance.
Shika Shika. Welcome home. I like you. I have to
tell you. Fanny. Panisse and Son. Birthday song.
To my wife. The thought of you. Love is a very
light thing. Other hands, other hearts. Be kind to
your parents.

Fanny.
Heritage LP-H   0055 (1954)
Cast: Harold Rome.
Credits: Music and lyrics, Harold Rome; book, S. N. Behr-
man and Joshua Logan; based on the trilogy by Marcel
Pagnol.

The Fantasticks. OC
MGM Records E/SE   3872 OC (1960)

Cast: Kenneth Nelson, Jerry Orbach, Rita Gardner, William
Larsen, Hugh Thomas.
Credits: Music, Harvey Schmidt; book and lyrics, Tom
Jones.
Songs: Try to remember. Much more. Metaphor. Never
say no. It depends on what you pay. You wonder how
these things begin. Soon it's gonna rain. Happy ending.
This plum is too ripe. I can see it. Plant a radish.
Round and round. There is a curious paradox. They
were you.

Fiddler on the roof. OC
RCA Victor LOC/LSO 1093 (1964)
Cast: Zero Mostel, Maria Karnilova, Beatrice Arthur.
Credits: Music, Jerry Bock; lyrics, Sheldon Harnick;
book, Joseph Stein; based on Sholem Aleichem's stories.
Songs: Tradition. Matchmaker, matchmaker. If I were a
rich man. Sabbath prayer. To life. Miracle of miracles.
Tevye's dream. Sunrise, sunset. Now I have everything.
Do you love me? Far from the home I love. Anatevka.

Fiddler on the roof. OC
Columbia SX 30742 (1971)
Cast: Topol, Miriam Karlin; original London cast.
Credits: Music, Jerry Bock; lyrics, Sheldon Harnick;
book, Joseph Stein; based on Sholem Aleichem's stories.

Fiddler on the roof.
London SP 44121 (1969)
Cast: Robert Merrill, Molly Picon.
Credits: Music, Jerry Bock; lyrics, Sheldon Harnick;
book, Joseph Stein; based on Sholem Aleichem's stories.
Songs: Tradition. If I were a rich man. Sabbath prayer.
Matchmaker. To life. Tevye's monologue. Miracle of
miracles. Sunrise, sunset. Far from the home I love.
Do you love me? Chava sequence. Anatevka.

Finian's rainbow. OC
RCA Victor LOC/LSO 1057 (1960)
Cast: Jeannie Carson, Howard Morris, Biff McGuire, Carol
Brice, Sorrell Booke, Bobby Howes.
Credits: Music, Burton Lane; lyrics, E. Y. Harburg; book,
E. Y. Harburg and Fred Saidy.
Songs: This time of year. How are things in Glocca Morra.
Look to the rainbow. Something sort of grandish. When
the idle poor become the idle rich. If this isn't love.
Old devil moon. Necessity. The begat. When I'm not
near the girl I love. The great come-and-get-it-day.

Finian's rainbow. OC
Columbia OL 4062/OS 2080 (1962)
Cast: Ella Logan, Donald Richards, David Wayne.
Credits: Music, Burton Lane; lyrics, E. Y. Harburg;
    book, E. Y. Harburg and Fred Saidy.

Fiorello. OC
Capitol WAO/SWAO 1321 (1959)
Cast: Tom Bosley, Patricia Wilson, Ellen Hanley, Howard
    Da Silva.
Credits: Music, Jerry Bock; lyrics, Sheldon Harnick;
    book, Jerome Weidman and George Abbott.
Songs: On the side of the angels. Politics and poker.
    Unfair. Marie's law. The name's La Guardia. The
    bum won. I love a cop. 'Til tomorrow. Home again.
    When did I fall in love. Gentleman Jimmy. Little tin
    box. The very next man.

First impressions. OC
Columbia OC 5400/OS 2014 (1959)
Cast: Polly Bergen, Hermione Gingold, Farley Granger.
Credits: Music and lyrics, George Weiss, Robert Goldman,
    and Glenn Paxton; book, Abe Burrows.
Songs: Five daughters. I'm me. Have you heard the news?
    A perfect evening. As long as there's a mother. Love
    will find out the way. A gentleman never falls wildly in
    love. Fragrant flower. I feel sorry for the girl. I
    suddenly find it agreeable. This really isn't me. Wasn't
    it a simply lovely wedding? A house in town. The heart
    has won the game. Let's fetch the carriage.

Flahooley. OC
Capitol T 11649 (1977)
Cast: Yma Sumac.
Credits: Music, Sammy Fain; lyrics, E. Y. Harburg;
    book, E. Y. Harburg and Fred Saidy.
Songs: You, too, can be a puppet. Here's to your illusions.
    B. G. Bigelow, Inc. Najala's lament. Who says there
    ain't no Santa Claus? Flahooley! The world is your
    balloon. Najala's song of joy. He's only wonderful.
    Jump, little chillun! Consternation. No more Flahooleys!
    Spirit of Capsulanti. Come back, little genie. Birds. The
    springtime cometh.

Flora the red menace. OC
RCA Victor LOC/LSO 1111 (1965); RCA ABL 1-2760 (1978)
Cast: Liza Minnelli, Bob Dishy.

Credits: Music, John Kander; lyrics, Fred Ebb; book, George Abbott and Robert Russell.
Songs: Unafraid. All I need. Not every day of the week. Sign here. The flame. Palomino pal. A quiet thing. Hello waves. Dear love. Express yourself. Knock knock. Sing happy. You are you.

Flower drum song. OC
Columbia OL 5350/OS 2009 (1959)
Cast: Pat Suzuki, Miyoshi Umeki, Juanita Hall.
Credits: Music, Richard Rodgers; lyrics, Oscar Hammerstein II; book, Oscar Hammerstein II and Joseph Fields.
Songs: You are beautiful. A hundred million miracles. I enjoy being a girl. I am going to like it here. Like a god. Chop suey. Don't marry me. Grant Avenue. Fan Tan Fannie. Gliding through my memoree. The other generation. Sunday.

Flower drum song. OC
Angel 35586/S35586 (1961)
Cast: Original London cast.
Credits: Music, Richard Rodgers; lyrics, Oscar Hammerstein II; book, Oscar Hammerstein II and Joseph Fields.

⚹Follies. OC
Capitol SO 761 (1971)
Cast: Gene Nelson, Alexis Smith, Dorothy Collins, John McMartin.
Credits: Music and lyrics, Stephen Sondheim; book, James Goldman.
Songs: Beautiful girls. Don't look at me. Waiting for the girls upstairs. Ah, Paris! Broadway baby. The road you didn't take. In Buddy's eyes. Who's that woman? I'm still here. Too many mornings. The right girl. Could I leave you? You're gonna love tomorrow. Love will see us through. The God-why-don't-you-love-me blues. Losing my mind. The story of Lucy and Jessie. Live, laugh, love.

Follies bergère. OC
Audio Fidelity AFSD 6135 (1964)
Cast: Patachou, Georges Ulmer.
Songs: Paris Bohème. Folle de Broadway. Bonjour Paris. Darling be careful. Quartier Latin. Mon manège a moi. Can can. Pigalle. What now my love? La musique.

Funny face. OC
Monmouth Evergreen MES 7037 (1971)

Cast: Adele Astaire, Fred Astaire.
Credits: Music, George Gershwin; lyrics, Ira Gershwin;
    book, Paul Gerard Smith and Fred Thompson.
Songs: Funny face.   He loves and she loves.   'S wonderful.
    High hat.   A few drinks.   My one and only.   Tell the
    doc.   The babbit and the bromide.

Funny girl.   OC
Capitol VAS/SVAS   2059 (1964)
Cast: Sydney Chaplin, Barbra Streisand.
Credits: Music, Jule Styne; lyrics, Robert Merrill;   book,
    Isobel Lennart.
Songs: If a girl isn't pretty.   I'm the greatest star.   Cornet
    man.   Who taught her everything.   His love makes me
    beautiful.   I want to be seen with you tonight.   Henry
    Street.   People.   You are woman.   Don't rain on my
    parade.   Sadie, Sadie.   Find yourself a man.   Rat-tat-tat-
    tat.   Who are you now?   The music that makes me dance.

A Funny thing happened on the way to the Forum.   OC
Capitol WAO/SWAO   1717 (1962)
Cast: Zero Mostel, Brian Davies, Jack Gilford, Preshy
    Marker.
Credits: Music and lyrics, Stephen Sondheim; book, Burt
    Shevelove and Larry Gelbart.
Songs: Comedy tonight.   Love, I hear.   Free.   Lovely.
    Pretty little picture.   Everybody ought to have a maid.
    I'm calm.   Impossible.   Bring me my bride.   That
    dirty old man.   That'll show him.

The Gay life.   OC
Capitol WAO/SWAO   1560 (1961)
Cast: Walter Chiari, Barbara Cook, Jules Munshin, Loring
    Smith.
Credits: Music and lyrics, Arthur Schwartz and Howard
    Dietz; book, Fay and Michael Kanin.
Songs: What a charming couple.   Why go anywhere at all?
    Bring your darling daughter.   Now I'm ready for a frau.
    Magic moment.   Who can?   You can.   Oh, mein liebchen.
    The label on the bottle.   This kind of girl.   The bloom
    is off the rose.   I'm glad I'm single.   Something you
    never had before.   You will never be lonely.   You're
    not the type.   Come a-wandering with me.   I never had
    a chance.   I wouldn't marry you.   From the first time.

Gentlemen prefer blondes.   OC
Columbia OL 4290 (1952); Columbia OS 2310 (1963);   Colum-
  bia S 32610 (1973)
Cast: Carol Channing, Yvonne Adair, Jack McCauley, Eric
  Brotherson, George S. Irving.
Credits: Music, Jule Styne; book, Joseph Fields and Anita
  Loos; lyrics, Leo Robin.
Songs: It's high time. Bye bye baby. A little girl from
  Little Rock. Just a kiss apart. I love what I'm doing.
  It's delightful down in Chile. You say you care. I'm
  a'tingle, I'm a'glow. Sunshine. Diamonds are a girl's
  best friend. Mamie is Mimi. Homesick blues. Keeping
  cool with Coolidge.

George M! OC
Columbia KOS 3200 (1968)
Cast: Joel Grey.
Credits: Music and lyrics, George M. Cohan; book, Michael
  Stewart and John and Fran Pascal; lyric and musical re-
  visions, Mary Cohan.
Songs: Musical moon. Oh, you wonderful boy. All aboard
  for Broadway. Musical comedy man. Twentieth century
  love. My town. Billie. Push me along in my push cart.
  Ring to the name of Rose. Popularity. Give my regards
  to Broadway. Forty-five minutes from Broadway. So
  long, Mary. Down by the Erie. Mary. All our friends.
  Yankee doodle dandy. Nellie Kelly, I love you. Harrigan.
  Over there. You're a grand old flag.

Gigi. OC
RCA Victor ABL 1-0404 (1973)
Cast: Alfred Drake, Agnes Moorehead, Maria Karnilova,
  Daniel Massey, Karin Wolfe.
Credits: Music, Frederick Loewe; lyrics, Alan Jay Lerner.
Songs: Thank heaven for little girls. It's a bore. The
  earth and other minor things. Paris is Paris again. She
  is not thinking of me. I remember it well. The night
  they invented champagne. Gigi. The contract. In this
  wide, wide world. I'm glad I'm not young anymore.

Gigi.
RCA Victor LPM/LSP 2275 (1960)
Cast: Jan Peerce, Robert Merrill, Jane Powell, Phil Harris.
Credits: Music, Frederick Loewe; lyrics, Alan Jay Lerner.

Girl crazy.
Columbia CL 822 (1956);   Columbia OL 7060/OS 2560 (1964);

CSP COS 2560 (1973)
Cast: Mary Martin.
Credits: Music, George Gershwin; lyrics, Ira Gershwin; book, Guy Bolton and Jack McGowan.
Songs: But not for me. Bidin' my time. Could you use me? Embraceable you. Treat me rough. I got rhythm. Bronco busters. Cactus time in Arizona. Sam and Delilah. Barbary Coast. Boy! What love has done to me.

The Girl in pink tights. OC
Columbia OL 4890 (1954)
Cast: Jeanmarie, Charles Goldner, David Atkinson, Alexandre Kalioujny, Brenda Lewis.
Credits: Music, Sigmund Romberg; lyrics, Leo Robin; book, Jerome Chodorov and Joseph Fields.
Songs: That naughty show from gay Paree. Lost in loveliness. I promised their mothers. Up in the elevated railway. In Paris and in love. You've got to be a little crazy. When am I free to love? Out of the way! Roll out the hose, boys. My heart won't say goodbye. We're all in the same boat. Love is the funniest thing. The cardinal's guard are we. Going to the devil.

The Girl who came to supper. OC
Columbia KOL 6020/KOS 2420 (1963)
Cast: José Ferrer, Florence Henderson.
Credits: Music and lyrics, Noël Coward; book, Harry Kurnitz.
Songs: I've been invited to a party. Lonely. This time it's true, love. I'll remember her. Here and now. My family tree. Soliloquies.

✳Godspell. OC
Bell 1102 (1971); Arista AL 4001 (1973)
Cast: David Haskell, Stephen Nathan.
Credits: Music and lyrics, Stephen Schwartz.
Songs: Prepare ye the way of the Lord. Save the people. Day by day. Learn your lessons well. Bless the Lord. All for the best. All good gifts. Light of the world. Turn back, O man. Alas for you. By my side. We beseech thee. On the willows.

The Golden apple. OC
RCA Victor LOC 1014 (1954); Elektra EKL 5000 (1961)
Cast: Priscilla Gillette, Stephen Douglass, Kaye Ballard, Jack Whiting.
Credits: Music, Jerome Moross; lyrics, John Latouche.

Golden boy. OC
Capitol VAS/SVAS 2124 (1964); Capitol STAO 11655 (1975)
Cast: Sammy Davis, Jr.
Credits: Music, Charles Strouse; book, Clifford Odets and
    William Gibson; lyrics, Lee Adams.
Songs: Workout. Night song. Everything's great. Gimme
    some. Stick around. Don't forget 127th Street. Lorna's
    here. This is the life. Golden boy. While the city
    sleeps. Colorful. I want to be with you. Can't you
    see it. No more.

Golden rainbow. OC
Calendar KOM/KOS 1001 (1968)
Cast: Eydie Gorme, Steve Lawrence.
Credits: Music, Walter Marks.

Goldilocks. OC
Columbia OL 5340/OS 2007 (1958); CSP 2007 (1973)
Cast: Don Ameche, Elaine Stritch, Russell Nype, Pat Stanley.
Credits: Music, Leroy Anderson; lyrics, Joan Ford, Walter
    and Jean Kerr; book, Walter and Jean Kerr.
Songs: Lazy moon. Give the little lady. Save a kiss. No
    one'll ever love you. Who's been sitting in my chair?
    There never was a woman. The pussy foot. Lady in
    waiting. The beast in you. Shall I take my heart and
    go? I can't be in love. Bad companions. I never know
    when. Two years in the making. Heart of stone.

Goodtime Charley. OC
RCA Red Seal ARL 1-1011 (1975)
Cast: Joel Grey, Ann Reinking.
Credits: Music, Larry Grossman; lyrics, Hal Hackady;
    book, Sidney Michaels.
Songs: Goodtime Charley. Voices and visions. Bits and
    pieces. To make the boy a man. Why can't we all be
    nice? Born lover. I am going to love (the man you're
    going to be). Castles of the Loire. You still have a
    long way to go. Confessional. One little year. I leave
    the world.

Grease. OC
MGM Records 1SE 34 OC (1972)
Cast: Barry Bostwick, Carole Demas.
Credits: Book, music, and lyrics, Warren Casey and Jim
    Jacobs.
Songs: Alma mater, Alma mater. Summer nights. Those
    magic changes. Freddy, my love. Greased lightnin'.

Mooning.   Look at me, I'm Sandra Dee.   We go together.
It's raining on prom night.   Born to hand-jive.   Beauty
school dropout.   Alone at a drive-in movie.   Rock 'n'
roll party queen.   There are worse things I could do.
All choked up.

※ Greenwillow.   OC
RCA Victor LOC/LSO   2001 (1960);   CSP P 13974 (1975)
Cast: Anthony Perkins.
Credits: Music and lyrics, Frank Loesser;   book, Lesser
Samuels and Frank Loesser.
Songs: A day borrowed from heaven.   The music of home.
Dorrie's wish.   Gideon Briggs, I love you.   Summertime
love.   Greenwillow walk.   Walking away whistling.   The
sermon.   Greenwillow Christmas.   Could've been a ring.
Never will I marry.   Faraway boy.   Clang dang the bell.
What a blessing.   He died good.   Summertime love.

Guys and dolls.   OC
Decca DL   9023 (1955);   Decca DL   79023 (1969);   MCA
Records MCA   2034 (1973)
Cast: Vivian Blaine, Robert Alda, Sam Levene.
Credits: Music and lyrics, Frank Loesser;   book, Jo Swerl-
ing and Abe Burrows; based on a story and characters by
Damon Runyon.
Songs: Runyonland music.   Fugue for tinhorns.   Follow the
fold.   The oldest established.   I'll know.   A bushel and
a peck.   Adelaide's lament.   Guys and dolls.   If I were
a bell.   My time of day.   I've never been in love before.
Take back your mink.   More I cannot wish you.   Luck
be a lady.   Sue me.   Sit down, you're rockin' the boat.
Marry the man today.

Guys and dolls.   OC
Motown M6 876S1 (1976)
Cast: Ernestine Jackson, Norman Donaldson, James Randolph,
Robert Guillaume.
Credits: Music and lyrics, Frank Loesser;   book, Joe Swerl-
ing and Abe Burrows;   based on a story and characters
by Damon Runyon.

Gypsy.   OC
Columbia OL 5420/OS   2017 (1959);   Columbia S   32607 (1973)
Cast: Ethel Merman, Jack Klugman, Sandra Church.
Credits: Music, Jule Styne;   book, Arthur Laurents;   lyrics,
Stephen Sondheim.
Songs: Let me entertain you.   Some people.   Small world.

Baby June and her newsboys. Mr. Goldstone, I love you.
Little lamb. You'll never get away from me. Dainty
June and her farmboys. If mama was married. All I
need is the girl. Everything's coming up roses. Together wherever we go. You gotta have a gimmick. Rose's
turn.

Gypsy. OC
RCA Victor LBL 1-5004 (1974)
Cast: Angela Lansbury, Barrie Ingham, Zan Charisse; orig-
inal London cast.
Credits: Music, Jule Styne; book, Arthur Laurents; lyrics,
Stephen Sondheim.

Gypsy Rose Lee remembers burlesque.
Stereoddities CG 1 (1962)
Cast: Gypsy Rose Lee.
Credits: Music, Bobby Kroll; book and lyrics, Eli Basse.

Hair. OC
RCA Victor LOC/LSO 1143 (1967); RCA ANL 1-0986 (1975)
Cast: Jonelle Allen, Ed Crowley, Walker Daniels, Jill
O'Hara, Gerome Ragni; original cast of the New York
Shakespeare Festival Public Theater.
Credits: Music, Galt MacDermott; book and lyrics, Gerome
Ragni and James Rado.
Songs: Ain't got no. I got life. Air. Going down. Hair.
Dead end. Frank Mills. Hare Krishna. Where do I go?
Electric blues. Easy to be hard. Manchester. White
boys. Black boys. Walking in space. Aquarius. Good
morning starshine. Exanaplanetooch. The climax.

Hair. OC
RCA Victor LOC/LSO 1150 (1968)
Cast: Lynn Kellogg, Gerome Ragni, James Rado, Steve
Curry, Ronald Dyson.
Credits: Music, Galt MacDermott; book and lyrics, Gerome
Ragni and James Rado.
Songs: Aquarius. Donna. Hashish. Sodomy. Colored
spade. Manchester England. I'm black. Ain't got no.
Air. Initials. I got life. Hair. My conviction. Don't
put it down. Frank Mills. Be-in. Where do I go?
Black boys. White boys. Easy to be hard. Walking in
space. Three-five-zero-zero. Abie baby. What a piece

of work is man.   Good morning starshine.   The flesh
failures.

Half a sixpence.   OC
RCA Victor LOC/LSO   1110 (1965)
Credits: Music and lyrics, David Heneker;   book, Beverly
Cross.

Half-past Wednesday.   OC
Columbia CL 1917/CS   8717 (1962)
Credits: Music, Robert Colby.

Hallelujah, baby.   OC
Columbia KOL 6690/KOS   3090 (1967)
Cast: Leslie Uggams, Robert Cooks, Allen Case.
Credits: Music, Jule Styne;   book, Arthur Laurents;   lyrics,
Betty Comden and Adolph Green.
Songs: My own morning.   The slice.   Feet do yo' stuff.
Watch my dust.   Smile, smile.   Witches' brew.   Being
good.   I wanted to change him.   Another day.   Talking
to yourself.   Hallelujah, baby!   Not mine.   I don't know
where she got it.   Now's the time.

A Hand is on the gate.
Verve Folkways FV/FVS   9040 OC (1966)
Cast: Leon Bibb, Cicely Tyson, Josephine Prémice, Roscoe
Lee Browne.
Songs: From the dark tower.   The negro speaks of rivers.
Frederick Douglass.   We wear the mask.   Runagate runa-
gate.   The dark symphony.   O black and unknown bards.
'Buked and scorned.   Ol' Lem.   Sonnet to a negro in
Harlem.   Southern mansion.   Mother to son.   Sence you
went away.   When Malindy sings.   A negro love song.
All hid.   Little boy.   An old woman remembers.   Be-
tween the world and me.   My angel.   Dink's song.   Jour-
ney to a parallel.   The end of man is his beauty.   The
ballad of Rudolph Reed.   A moment please.   We have
been believers.   O' Shenandoah.   La vie, c'est la vie.
At early morn.   The elevator man.   Look at that gal.
Glory, glory.   To a young poet.   Bound no'th blues.   Ma
Rainey.   Get up blues.   The rebel.   Distant drum.   No
images.   Why try.   Ontogeny recapitulates.   Robert Whit-
more.   Harlem sweeties.   A street in Bronzeville.   After
winter.   When in Rome.   American gothic.   Jane Jane.
Epigram.   Conception.   Alien.   My Lord, what a morning.
The preacher ruminates.   Personal.   Preface to a 20 vol-
ume suicide note.   Careless love.   This ain't no mass
thing.   Rocks and gravel.   If the birds.

The Happiest girl in the world.   OC
Columbia KOL 5650/KOS   2050 (1961)
Cast: Cyril Ritchard.
Credits: Music, Robert De Cormier and Jay Gurney, adapted
   from the music of Jacques Offenbach;   lyrics, E. Y. Har-
   burg;   book, Fred Saidy and Henry Myers.

Happy end.
Columbia OL   5630 (1964)
Cast: Lotte Lenya.
Credits: Music, Kurt Weill;   lyrics, Bertolt Brecht.

The Happy time.   OC
RCA Victor LOC/LSO   1144 (1968)
Cast: Robert Goulet, David Wayne.
Credits: Music, John Kander;   lyrics, Fred Ebb;   book,
   N. Richard Nash.
Songs: The happy time.   He's back.   Catch my garter.
   Tomorrow morning.   Please stay.   I don't remember you.
   St. Pierre.   Without me.   Among my yesterdays.   The
   life of the party.   Seeing things.   A certain girl.

Hazel Flagg,   OC
RCA Victor LOC   1010 (1953);   RCA Red Seal CBM 1-2207
   (1977)
Cast: Helen Gallagher, Thomas Mitchell, Benay Venuta,
   John Howard.
Credits: Music, Jule Styne;   lyrics, Bob Hilliard;   book,
   Ben Hecht.
Songs: A little more heart.   The world is beautiful today.
   The Rutland bounce.   I'm glad I'm leaving.   Hello, Hazel.
   Every street's a boulevard in old New York.   How do you
   speak to an angel?   Autograph chant.   I feel like I'm
   gonna live forever.   You're gonna dance with me, Willie.
   Who is the bravest?   Salomee.   Everybody loves to take
   a bow.   Laura de Maupassant.

Hello Dolly.   OC
RCA Victor LOC/LSO   1087 (1964)
Cast: Carol Channing, David Burns.
Credits: Music and lyrics, Jerry Herman;   book, Michael
   Stewart;   based on The matchmaker, by Thornton Wilder.
Songs: I put my hand in.   It takes a woman.   Put on your
   Sunday clothes.   Ribbons down my back.   Motherhood.
   Dancing.   Before the parade passes by.   Elegance.   Hello,
   Dolly.   It only takes a moment.   So long dearie.

Hello, Dolly.   OC
RCA Victor LOCD/LSOD   2007 (1965)
Cast: Mary Martin;   original London cast.
Credits: Music and lyrics, Jerry Herman;   book, Michael
   Stewart;   based on The matchmaker, by Thornton Wilder.

Hello, Dolly.   OC
RCA Victor LSO   1147 (1967);   RCA ANL   1-2849 (1977)
Cast: Pearl Bailey, Cab Calloway.
Credits: Music and lyrics, Jerry Herman;   book, Michael
   Stewart; based on The matchmaker, by Thornton Wilder.

Hello, Solly!   OC
Capitol W/SW   2731 (1967)
Cast: Mickey Katz.

Here's love.   OC
Columbia KOL 6000/KOS   2400 (1963)
Cast: Janis Paige, Craig Stevens, Laurence Naismith.
Credits: Music and lyrics, Meredith Willson.
Songs: Here's love.   My wish.   My state.   My Kansas, my
   home.   Love, come take me again.   Pine cones and holly
   berries.

High button shoes.   OC
RCA Camden CAL   457 (1958);   RCA Victor LOC/LSO   1107
   (1965)
Cast: Phil Silvers, Nanette Fabray.
Credits: Music, Jule Styne;   lyrics, Sammy Cahn;   book,
   Stephen Longstreet.

High spirits.   OC
ABC-Paramount ABC-OC   1 (1964)
Cast: Beatrice Lillie, Tammy Grimes, Edward Woodward.
Credits: Music, lyrics, and book, Hugh Martin and Timothy
   Gray;   based on Blithe spirit, by Noël Coward.
Songs: You'd better love me.   Where is the man I married?
   Was she prettier than I?   Home sweet heaven.   If I gave
   you.   Forever and a day.

House of flowers.
Columbia OL   4969 (1955);   Columbia OS   2320 (1963);   CSP
   COS   2320 (1973)
Cast: Pearl Bailey, Danny Carroll.
Credits: Music, Harold Arlen;   book, Truman Capote;   lyrics,
   Truman Capote and Harold Arlen.
Songs: Waitin'.   One man ain't quite enough.   A sleepin' bee.

Bamboo cage. House of flowers. Two ladies in de shade
of de banana tree. What is a friend for? Slide "boy",
slide. I'm gonna leave off wearing my shoes. Has I let
you down? I never has seen snow. Don't like goodbyes.
Mardi gras.

How now, Dow Jones. OC
RCA Victor LOC/LSO 1142 (1968)
Cast: Anthony Roberts, Marlyn Mason, Brenda Vaccaro,
Hiram Sherman.
Credits: Music, Elmer Bernstein; lyrics, Carolyn Leigh;
book, Max Shulman.
Songs: A-B-C. They don't make 'em like that anymore.
Live a little. The pleasure's about to be mine. A little
investigation. Walk away. Gawk, tousle and shucks.
Shakespeare lied. Step to the rear. Big trouble. Rich
is better. Just for the moment. He's here. Touch and
go.

How to steal an election. OC
RCA Victor LSO 1153 (1968)
Cast: D.R. Allen, Clifton Davis, Carole Demas.
Credits: Music and lyrics, Oscar Brand; book, William F.
Brown.

How to succeed in business without really trying. OC
RCA Victor LOC/LSO 1066 (1961)
Cast: Robert Morse, Rudy Vallee, Bonnie Scott, Virginia
Martin, Charles Nelson Reilly.
Credits: Music and lyrics, Frank Loesser; book, Abe
Burrows, Jack Weinstock, and Willie Gilbert; based on
How to succeed in business without really trying, by
Shepherd Mead.
Songs: How to. Happy to keep his dinner warm. Coffee
break. The company way. A secretary is not a toy.
Been a long day. Grand old ivy. Paris original. Rose-
mary. Cinderella, darling. Love from a heart of gold.
I believe in you. Brotherhood of man.

I can get it for you wholesale. OC
Columbia KOL 5780/KOS 2180 (1962)
Cast: Lillian Roth, Jack Kruschen, Harold Lang, Ken Le
Roy, Marilyn Cooper, Barbra Streisand, Bambi Linn,
Elliott Gould.

Credits: Music and lyrics, Harold Rome;   book, Jerome
Weidman.
Songs: I'm not a well man.   The way things are.   When
gemini meets capricorn.   Momma, Momma.   The sound
of money.   Too soon.   The family way.   Who knows?
Ballad of the garment trade.   Have I told you lately?   A
gift today.   Miss Marmelstein.   A funny thing happened.
What's in it for me?   Eat a little something.   What are
they doing to us now?

I do!   I do!   OC
RCA Victor LOC/LSO   1128 (1967)
Cast: Mary Martin, Robert Preston.
Credits: Music, Harvey Schmidt;   book and lyrics, Tom
Jones;   based on The fourposter, by Jan de Hartog.
Songs: All the dearly beloved.   Together forever.   I do!
I do!   Goodnight.   I love my wife.   Something has hap-
pened.   My cup runneth over.   Love isn't everything.
Nobody's perfect.   A well known fact.   Flaming Agnes.
The honeymoon is over.   Where are the snows?   When
the kids get married.   The father of the bride.   What
is a woman?   Someone needs me.   Roll up the ribbons.
This house.

I had a ball.   OC
Mercury OCM 2210/OCS   6210 (1965)
Cast: Buddy Hackett, Richard Kiley.
Credits: Music, Stan Freeman;   lyrics, Jack Lawrence;
book, Jerome Chodorov.
Songs: Garside the Great.   Coney Island, U. S. A.   The
other half of me.   Addie's at it again.   I've got everything I want.   Dr. Freud.   Think beautiful.   Faith.   Can
it be possible?   Neighbourhood.   The affluent society.   I
had a ball.   Almost.   Fickle finger of fate.   You deserve me.

I love my wife.   OC
Atlantic SD   19107 (1977)
Cast: Lenny Baker, Joanna Gleason, Ilene Graff, James
Naughton.
Credits: Music, Cy Coleman;   book and lyrics, Michael
Stewart.
Songs: We're still friends.   Monica.   By threes.   Love
revolution.   A mover's life.   Someone wonderful I missed.
Sexually free.   Hey there, good times.   By the way if
you are free tonight.   Lovers on Christmas Eve.   Scream.
Ev'rybody today is turning on.   Married couple seeks mar-
ried couple.   I love my wife.   In conclusion.

I married an angel.
Pelican LP 103 (1973)
Cast: Jeanette MacDonald, Nelson Eddy.
Credits: Music, Richard Rodgers; lyrics, Lorenz Hart;
book, Richard Rodgers and Lorenz Hart.
Songs: May I present the girl. I married an angel. A
twinkle in your eye. I'll tell the man in the street.

In circles. OC
Avant Garde AV 108 (1968)
Cast: Theo Barnes, Jacque Lynn Colton.
Credits: Music, Al Carmines; book, Gertrude Stein.

Inner city. OC
RCA Victor LSO 1171 (1972)
Credits: Music, Helen Miller; lyrics, E. Merriam.

Ipi-Tombi. OC
Ashtree ASH 26000 (1975)
Cast: South Africa cast recording.
Credits: Music, Bertha Eguos; lyrics, Gail Lakier.
Songs: Ipi-Tombi. Thando je phelile. Korbosha. Andy's
song. Moriva. Hakelejeje. Bona noga. Egoli.
Emdudeni. The click. Baby baby. Wishing. Ndoba
sathi nina. Shosholoza. The digger. The warrior.
Bayete.

Irene. OC
Columbia KS 32266 (1973)
Cast: Debbie Reynolds, Monte Markham, George S. Irving,
Ruth Warrick, Patsy Kelly.
Credits: Music, Harry Tierney; book, Hugh Wheeler and
Joseph Stein; lyrics, Joseph McCarthy.
Songs: The world must be bigger than an avenue. What do
you want to make those eyes at me for? The family tree.
Alice blue gown. They go wild, simply wild over me.
An Irish girl. Mother, angel, darling. The Riviera rage.
I'm always chasing rainbows. The last part of ev'ry
party. We're getting away with it. Irene. The great
lover tango. You made me love you.

Irene. OC
Monmouth-Evergreen MES 7057 (1974)
Cast: Edith Day; original 1920 London cast.
Credits: Music, Harry Tierney; book, James Montgomery;
lyrics, Joseph McCarthy.

Irma la douce. OC
Columbia OL 5560/OS   2029 (1960)
Cast: Elizabeth Seal, Keith Michell.
Credits: Music, Marguerite Monnot;   original book and
   lyrics, Alexandre Breffort;   English book and lyrics,
   Julian More, David Heneker, and Monty Norman.
Songs: Valse milieu.   Sons of France.   The bridge of
   Caulaincourt.   Our language of love.   She's got the lot.
   Dis-donc, dis-donc.   Le grisbi is le root of le evil in
   man.   The wreck of a Mec.   That's a crime.   From a
   prison cell.   Irma-la-douce.   There is only one Paris
   for that.   But.   Christmas child.

Isabel's a jezebel.   OC
Kilmarnock KIL-72006 (1974)
Cast: Original London cast.
Credits: Music, Galt MacDermott;   lyrics, William Dumaresq.
Songs: More than earth, more than air.   Down by the ocean.
   Oh fish in the sea.   On the sand by the sea.   Isabel's a
   Jezebel.   In another life.   Nothing.   Sand.   Oh mummy
   darling.   Love knows no season.   So ends our night.   The
   saddest moon.   Mama don't want no baby.   These are the
   things.   Stanley irritability.   Use my name.   The moon
   should be rising soon.   The weeds in the wind: My God
   when I think.   Hah.

It's a bird, it's a plane, it's Superman.   OC
Columbia KOL 6570/KOS   2970 (1966)
Cast: Jack Cassidy.
Credits: Music, Charles Strouse;   lyrics, Lee Adams;   book,
   David Newman and Robert Benton.
Songs: Doing good.   We need him.   It's Superman.   We don't
   matter at all.   Revenge.   The woman for the man.   You've
   got possibilities.   What I've always wanted.   Everything's
   easy when you know how.   It's supernice.   So long, big
   guy.   The strongest man in the world.   Ooh, do you love
   you!   You've got what I need.   I'm not finished yet!   Pow!
   Bam!   Zonk!

Jacques Brel is alive and well and living in Paris.   OC
Columbia D2S   779 (1968)
Cast: Elly Stone, Mort Shuman, Shaun Elliott, Alice Whit-
   field.
Credits: Music, Jacques Brel;   English lyrics based on Brel's

lyrics and additional material by Eric Blau and Mort Shuman.
Songs: Marathon. Alone. Madeleine. I loved. Mathilde. Bachelor's dance. Timid Frieda. My death. Jackie. Desperate ones. Sons of.... Amsterdam. The bulls. Old folks. Marieke. Brussels. Fanette. Funeral tango. You're not alone. Next. Carousel. If we only have love.

Jacques Brel is alive and well and living in Paris.   OC
Playhouse Square Records PHS CLE 2S   101 (1974)
Cast: Cliff Bemis, David O. Frazier, Providence Hollander, Theresa Piteo; original Cleveland cast.
Credits: Music, Jacques Brel; English lyrics based on Brel's lyrics and additional material by Eric Blau and Mort Shuman.

Jamaica.   OC
RCA Victor LOC/LSO   1036 (1957);   LOC/LSO   1103 (1965)
Cast: Lena Horne, Ricardo Montalban.
Credits: Music, Harold Arlen; lyrics, E. Y. Harburg;   book, E. Y. Harburg and Fred Saidy.
Songs: Cocoanut sweet. Take it slow, Joe. Ain't it the truth? Push the button. Leave the atom alone. Napoleon. Savannah. Little biscuit. Incompatibility.

Jennie.   OC
RCA Victor LOC/LSO   1083 (1963)
Cast: Mary Martin.
Credits: Music, Arthur Schwartz;   lyrics, Howard Dietz.

Jesus Christ superstar.
Decca DXSA   7206 (1970);   MCA Records MCA   2-10000 (1973)
Cast: Murray Head, Ian Gillan.
Credits: Music, Andrew Lloyd Webber; lyrics, Tim Rice.
Songs: Heaven on their minds. Everything's alright. This Jesus must die. Hosanna. Pilate's dream. I don't know how to love him. Gethsemane. King Herod's song. Could we start again please. Judas' death. Trial before Pilate. Superstar. John nineteen: forty-one.

Jesus Christ superstar.   OC
MCA Records MCA   5000 (1973)
Cast: Ben Vereen, Jeff Fenholt.
Credits: Music, Andrew Lloyd Webber; lyrics, Tim Rice.

Jesus Christ superstar.
Super Majestic SBBH 1. 610 (1973)
Cast: Sammy Turner, Sam Taylor, Jr. , Jaye Kennedy,
   J. D. Bryant.
Credits: Music, Andrew Lloyd Webber; lyrics, Tim Rice.

Jimmy. OC
RCA Victor LSO 1162 (1970)
Cast: Frank Gorshin, Anita Gillette, Julie Wilson.
Credits: Music and lyrics, Bill and Patti Jacob; book,
   Melville Shavelson; based on the novel Beau James, by
   Gene Fowler.
Songs: Will you think of me tomorrow?   The little woman.
   The darlin' of New York.   Oh, gee! The Walker walk.
   That old familiar ring.   I only wanna laugh.   Riverside
   Drive.   What's out there for me?   The squabble song.
   One in a million.   It's a nice place to visit.   The charm-
   in' son-of-a-bitch.   Jimmy.   Life is a one way street.
   Our Jimmy.

Joy. OC
RCA Victor LSO 1166 (1970)
Cast: Oscar Brown, Jean Pace, Sivuca.
Credits: Music and lyrics, Oscar Brown.
Songs: Time.   What is a friend?   Funny feelin?   Under
   the sun.   Wimmen's ways.   Brown baby.   Mother Africa's
   day.   A new generation.   Sky and sea.   If I only had.
   Nothing but a fool.   Much as I love you.   Afro blue.
   Funky world.

Jubalay. OC
Jubalay Productions JP 9001 (1974)
Cast: Brent Carver, Ruth Nichol, Patrick Rose, Diane
   Stapley; original Vancouver cast.
Credits: Music and lyrics, Patrick Rose and Merv Campone.
Songs: Jubalay.   Craftsman.   Bring back swing.   Yesterday's
   lover.   CNR.   Wailing wall.   Dewey and Sal.   Sailor.
   Find me.   His name is love.   La belle province.   Lullabye.

Jubilee.
Columbia KS 31456 (1972)
Includes Cole Porter's recollections of moments and notables
   in his career.
Cast: Mary Martin, Danny Kaye, Ethel Merman, Cole Porter.
Credits: Music and lyrics, Cole Porter.
Songs: A picture of me without you.   Entrance of Eric.   The
   Kling-kling bird on the divi-divi tree.   When love comes
   your way.   What a nice municipal park.   When me, Mow-

gli, love. Ev'rybod-ee who's anybod-ee. Sunday morning, breakfast time. Me and Marie. My heart belongs to daddy. Most gentlemen don't like love. Let's not talk about love. Farming. You're the top. I get a kick out of you.

Juno. OC
Columbia OL 5380/OS 2013 (1959)
Cast: Shirley Booth, Melvyn Douglas.
Credits: Music and lyrics, Marc Blitzstein; book, Joseph Stein.

Kean. OC
Columbia KOL 5720/KOS 2120 (1961)
Cast: Alfred Drake.
Credits: Music and lyrics, Robert Wright and George Forrest; book, Peter Stone.

The King and I.
Columbia OL 8040/OS 2640 (1964)
Cast: Barbara Cook, Theodore Bikel.
Credits: Music, Richard Rodgers; book and lyrics, Oscar Hammerstein II.
Songs: I whistle a happy tune. My lord and master. Hello, young lovers. March of the Siamese children. A puzzlement. Getting to know you. We kiss in a shadow. Shall I tell you what I think of you? Something wonderful. Western people funny. I have dreamed. Song of the King. Shall we dance?

The King and I. OC
Decca DL 9008 (1957); MCA Records MCA 2028 (1973)
Cast: Gertrude Lawrence, Yul Brenner.
Credits: Music, Richard Rodgers; book and lyrics, Oscar Hammerstein II.

The King and I. OC
RCA Victor LOC/LSO 1092 (1964)
Cast: Risë Stevens, Darren McGavin; original cast from the Music Theater of Lincoln Center.
Credits: Music, Richard Rodgers; book and lyrics, Oscar Hammerstein II.

Kismet. OC
Columbia OL 4850 (1954); Columbia OS 2060 (1962); Columbia S 32605 (1973)
Cast: Alfred Drake, Doretta Morrow, Joan Diener, Henry Calvin, Richard Kiley.

46   The Broadway Musical

Credits: Musical themes, Alexander Borodin; musical adaptation and lyrics, Robert Wright and George Forrest;
book, Charles Lederer and Luther Davis.
Songs: Sands of time.   Rhymes have I.   Fate.   Bazaar of
the caravans.   Not since Nineveh.   Baubles, bangles and
beads.   Stranger in paradise.   He's in love!   Gesticulate.
Night of my nights.   Was I wazir?   Rahadlakum.   And this
is my beloved.   The olive tree.   Zubbediya.   Samaris' dance.

Kismet.   OC
RCA Victor LOC/LSO   1112 (1965)
Cast: Alfred Drake, Anne Jeffreys, Lee Venora;   original
cast from the Music Theater of Lincoln Center.
Credits: Musical themes, Alexander Borodin;   musical adap-
tation and lyrics, Robert Wright and George Forrest;   book,
Charles Lederer and Luther Davis.

Kismet.
London SP   44043 (1964)
Cast: Robert Merrill, Regina Resnik, Kenneth McKellar.
Credits: Musical themes, Alexander Borodin;   musical adap-
tation and lyrics, Robert Wright and George Forrest; book,
Charles Lederer and Luther Davis.

Kismet.
Angel S   37321 (1978)
Cast: Dorothy Kirsten, Gordon MacRae.
Credits: Musical themes, Alexander Borodin;   musical adap-
tation and lyrics, Robert Wright and George Forrest;   book,
Charles Lederer and Luther Davis.

Kiss me, Kate.   OC
Columbia OL   4140 (1950);   Columbia OS   2300 (1963);   Co-
lumbia S   32609 (1973)
Cast: Alfred Drake, Patricia Morison, Lisa Kirk.
Credits: Music and lyrics, Cole Porter;   book, Bella and
Samuel Spewack.
Songs: Another op'nin', another show.   Why can't you be-
have?   Wunderbar.   So in love.   We open in Venice.
Tom, Dick or Harry.   I've come to wive it wealthily in
Padua.   I hate men.   Were thine that special face.   Too
darn hot.   Where is the life that late I led?   Always true
to you.   Bianca.   Brush up your Shakespeare.   I am
ashamed that women are so simple.   So kiss me, Kate.

Kiss me, Kate.
Capitol TAO/STAO   1267 (1959)
Cast: Alfred Drake, Patricia Morison.

Credits: Music/lyrics, Cole Porter; book, B. and S. Spewack.

Kiss me, Kate.
Columbia CL 1768/CS 8568 (1962)
Cast: Earl Wrightson, Lois Hunt, Mary Mayo.
Credits: Music and lyrics, Cole Porter; book, Bella and
Samuel Spewack.

Kiss me, Kate.
RCA Victor LPM 1984 (1959)
Cast: Gogi Grant, Howard Keel, Anne Jeffreys.
Credits: Music and lyrics, Cole Porter; book, Bella and
Samuel Spewack.

Kwamina. OC
Capitol WAO/SWAO 1645 (1961)
Cast: Sally Ann Howes; Terry Carter, Brock Peters.
Credits: Music/lyrics, Richard Adler; book, Robert A. Aurthur.
Songs: The cocoa bean song. Welcome home. The sun is
beginning to crow. Did you hear that? You're as English
as. Seven sheep, four red shirts, and a bottle of gin.
Nothing more to look forward to. What's wrong with me?
Something big. Ordinary people. A man can have no
choice. What happened to me tonight? One wife. Another
time, another place.

Lady be good. OC
Monmouth-Evergreen MES 7036 (1971)
Cast: Adele Astaire, Fred Astaire.
Credits: Music, George Gershwin; lyrics, Ira Gershwin;
book, Guy Bolton and Fred Thompson.
Songs: Oh lady be good. Hang on to me. Fascinating
rhythm. I'd rather Charleston. So am I. Half of it
dearie blues. Swiss maid. The following songs are also
included: Not my girl. Louisiana. Puttin' on the ritz.
Crazy feet. Night and day. After you, who. Flyin' down
to Rio. Music makes me.

Lady in the dark. OC
Columbia OL 5990/OS 2390 (1963); CSP COS 2390 (1973)
Cast: Risë Stevens, Adolph Green, John Reardon.
Credits: Music, Kurt Weill; lyrics, Ira Gershwin; book,
Moss Hart.
Songs: Oh fabulous one. Huxley. One life to live. Girl of the
moment. Mapleton High chorale. This is new. The princess
of pure delight. The greatest show on earth. The best years
of his life. Tschaikowsky. The saga of Jenny. My ship.

Lady in the dark.
RCA Victor LM 1882 (1954)
Cast: Ann Sothern, Carleton Carpenter.
Credits: Music, Kurt Weill; lyrics, Ira Gershwin; book,
   Moss Hart.

Lady in the dark.
RCA Victor LPV   503 (1964)
Cast: Gertrude Lawrence.
Credits: Music, Kurt Weill; lyrics, Ira Gershwin; book,
   Moss Hart.

The Last sweet days of Isaac.   OC
RCA Victor LSO   1169 (1970)
Cast: Austin Pendleton, Fredericka Weber.
Credits: Music, Nancy Ford; book and lyrics, Gretchen
   Cryer.
Songs: A transparent crystal moment.   My most important mo-
   ments go by.   Love, you come to me.   I want to walk to San
   Francisco.   I can't live in solitary.   Herein lie the seeds
   of revolution.   Touching your hand is like touching your
   mind.   Somebody died today.   Yes, I know that I'm alive.

Let it ride.   OC
RCA Victor LOC/LSO   1064 (1961)
Cast: George Gobel, Sam Levene, Barbara Nichols.
Credits: Music, Jay Livingston; lyrics, Ray Evans.

Let my people come.   OC
Libra Records LR   1069 (1974)
Credits: Music, Earl Wilson Jr.; lyrics, Earl Wilson Jr.
   and Phil Oesterman.
Songs: Give it to em.   I'm gay.   Come in my mouth.   Dirty
   words.   Linda, Georgina, Marilyn & me.   I believe my
   body.   Take me home with you.   Choir practice.   And
   she loved me.   Whatever turns you on.   Doesn't anybody
   love anymore.   Let my people come.

L'il Abner.   OC
Columbia OL   5150 (1957)
Cast: Edith Adams, Peter Palmer.
Credits: Music, Gene De Paul; lyrics, Johnny Mercer;
   book, Norman Panama and Melvin Frank.
Songs: A typical day.   If I had my druthers.   Jubilation T.
   Cornpone.   Rag offen the bush.   Namely you.   Unnecessary
   town.   The country's in the very best of hands.   Oh, happy
   day.   I'm past my prime.   Love in a home.   Progress is

the root of all evil.   Put 'em back.   The matrimonial
stomp.

Little Mary Sunshine. OC
Capitol WAO/SWAO 1240 (1960)
Cast: Eileen Brennan.
Credits: Book, music, and lyrics, Rick Besoyan.

✕ Little me. OC
RCA Victor LOC/LSO 1078 (1962)
Cast: Sid Caesar, Virginia Martin, Nancy Andrews.
Credits: Music, Cy Coleman; lyrics, Carolyn Leigh; book,
   Neil Simon.
Songs: The truth. The other side of the tracks. I love
   you. Deep down inside. Be a performer. Dimples.
   Boom-boom. I've got your number. Real live girl. Poor
   little Hollywood star. Little me. Goodbye. Here's to
   us.

A Little night music. OC
Columbia KS 32265 (1973)
Cast: Glynis Johns, Len Cariou, Hermione Gingold.
Credits: Music and lyrics, Stephen Sondheim; book, Hugh
   Wheeler.
Songs: Now. Later. Soon. The glamorous life. Remember? You must meet my wife. Liaisons. In praise of
   women. Every day a little death. A weekend in the
   country. The sun won't set. It would have been wonderful. Perpetual anticipation. Send in the clowns. The
   miller's son.

A Little night music. OC
RCA Red Seal LRL 1-5090 (1975)
Cast: Jean Simmons, Hermione Gingold, Jose Ackland,
   David Kernan; original London cast.
Credits: Music and lyrics, Stephen Sondheim; book, Hugh
   Wheeler.

The Littlest revue. OC
Epic LN 3275 (1956)
Credits: Music, Vernon Duke; lyrics, Ogden Nash.

Lorelei. OC
MGM Records MV 5097 OC (1973)
Cast: Carol Channing.
Credits: Music, Jule Styne; lyrics, Betty Comden and Adolph
   Green; book, Kenny Solms and Gail Parent.

Songs: Looking back. Bye bye baby. It's high time. A
   little girl from Little Rock. I love what I'm doing. I'm
   a'tingle, I'm a'glow. Keeping cool with Coolidge. Paris,
   Paris. I won't let you get away. Mamie is Mimi. Lorelei. Homesick blues. Just a kiss apart. Diamonds are
   a girl's best friend.

Lost in the stars. OC
Decca 8028 (1951);   MCA Records MCA 2071 (1973)
Cast: Todd Duncan, Inez Matthews, Frank Roane.
Credits: Music, Kurt Weill; book, Maxwell Anderson; based
   on Cry, the beloved country, by Alan Paton.
Songs: The hills of Ixopo. Thousands of miles. Train to
   Johannesburg. The little gray house. Who'll buy. Trou-
   ble man. Murder in Parkwold. Fear. Lost in the stars.
   O Tixo, Tixo, help me. Stay well. Cry, the beloved
   country. Big Mole. A bird of passage.

Mack & Mabel. OC
ABC Records ABCH 830 (1974)
Cast: Robert Preston, Bernadette Peters, Lisa Kirk.
Credits: Music and lyrics, Jerry Herman.
Songs: Movies were movies. Look what happened to Mabel.
   Big time. I won't send roses. I wanna make the world
   laugh. Wherever he ain't. Hundreds of girls. When
   Mabel comes in the room. My heart leaps up. Time
   heals everything. Tap your troubles away. I promise
   you a happy ending.

The Mad show. OC
Columbia OL 6530/OS 2930 (1966)
Credits: Music, Mary Rodgers; lyrics, Marshall Barer,
   Larry Siegel, and Steven Vinaver; book, Larry Siegel
   and Stan Hart.

Maggie Flynn. OC
RCA Victor LSOD 2009 (1969)
Credits: Music and lyrics, George D. Weiss and Hugo &
   Luigi.

The Magic show. OC
Bell 9003 (1974)
Cast: Cheryl Barnes, Annie McGreevey, Dale Soules, David
   Ogden Stiers.

Credits: Music and lyrics, Stephen Schwartz; book, Bob
  Randall.
Songs: Up to his old tricks. Solid silver platform shoes.
  Lion tamer. Style. Two's company. Charmin's lament.
  The Goldfarb variations. West end avenue. Sweet, sweet,
  sweet. Before your very eyes.

Maid of the mountains. OC
Odeon SCX 6504 (1972)
Cast: Original London cast.
Credits: Music, Harold Fraser-Simson; lyrics, Harry
  Graham; book, Frederick Lonsdale.

Make a wish.
RCA CBM 1-2033 (1976)
Cast: Nanette Fabray, Harold Lang.
Credits: Music and lyrics, Hugh Martin; book, Preston
  Sturges; based on The good fairy, by Ferenc Molnar.
Songs: That face. When does this feeling go away? What
  I was warned about. Over and over. Paris, France.
  The tour must go on. I wanna be good 'n' bad. Suits
  me fine. Hello, hello, hello. Tonight you are in Paree.
  Who gives a sou? Make a wish. I'll never make a
  Frenchman out of you. Take me back to Texas with you.

Mame. OC
Columbia KOL 6600/KOS 3000 (1966)
Cast: Angela Lansbury.
Credits: Music and lyrics, Jerry Herman; book, Jerome
  Lawrence and Robert E. Lee.
Songs: St. Bridget. It's today. Open a new window. The
  man in the moon. My best girl. We need a little Christ-
  mas. Mame. The letter. Bosom buddies. Gooch's
  song. That's how young I feel. If he walked into my life.

Man of La Mancha. OC
Kapp KRL/KRS 5505 (1965); MCA Records MCA 2018 (1973)
Cast: Richard Kiley, Irving Jacobson, Joan Diener.
Credits: Music, Mitch Leigh; lyrics, Joe Darion; book,
  Dale Wasserman.
Songs: Man of La Mancha. It's all the same. Dulcinea.
  I'm only thinking of him. I really like him. What do
  you want of me? The barber's song. Golden helmet.
  To each his Dulcinea. The impossible dream. Little
  bird, little bird. The dubbing. The abduction. Aldonza.
  A little gossip.

Man of La Mancha.
Columbia S 31237 (1972)
Cast: Jim Nabors, Marilyn Horne, Jack Gilford, Richard
    Tucker.
Credits: Music, Mitch Leigh; lyrics, Joe Darion; book,
    Dale Wasserman.

Man of La Mancha. OC
Decca DXS 7203 (1968); MCA Records MCA 10010 (1975)
Cast: Keith Michell, Joan Diener; original London cast.
Credits: Music, Mitch Leigh; lyrics, Joe Darion; book,
    Dale Wasserman.

Man with a load of mischief. OC
Kapp KRL 5508 (1966)
Credits: Music, John Clifton.

Me and Bessie.
Columbia PC 34032 (1976)
Cast: Linda Hopkins.
Songs: I'm not Bessie. Gimme a pigfoot. Romance in the
    dark. Preachin' the blues. A good man is hard to find.
    'Tain't nobody's bizness if I do. Put it right here. You've
    been a good old wagon. After you've gone. Empty bed
    blues. Kitchen man. Fare thee well. Nobody knows you
    when you're down and out. Trouble.

Me and Juliet. OC
RCA Victor LOC/LSO 1098 (1964)
Cast: Joan McCracken.
Credits: Music, R. Rodgers; lyrics, O. Hammerstein II.
Songs: No other love. Marriage-type love. Keep it gay.
    I'm your girl. We deserve each other. It's me.

The Me nobody knows. OC
Atlantic SD 1566 (1970)
Credits: Music, Gary William Friedman; lyrics, Will Holt.
Songs: Dream babies. Light sings. This world. How I feel. The
    white horse. If I had a million dollars. Sounds. The tree.
    Something beautiful. Black. War babies. Let me come in.

Milk and honey. OC
RCA Victor LOC/LSO 1065 (1961)
Cast: Robert Weede, Mimi Benzell, Molly Picon.
Credits: Music and lyrics, Jerry Herman; book, Don Appell.
Songs: Shalom. Independence Day hora. Milk and honey.
    There's no reason in the world. Chin up, ladies. That
    was yesterday. Let's not waste a moment. The wedding.

Like a young man.   I will follow you.   Hymn to Hymie.
As simple as that.

Miss Liberty.   OC
Columbia OL 4220 (1951);   CSP AOL 4220 (1972)
Cast: Eddie Albert, Allyn McLerie, Mary McCarty.
Credits: Music/lyrics, Irving Berlin; book, Robert Sherwood.
Songs: I'd like my picture took.   The most expensive statue
in the world.   Little fish in a big pond.   Let's take an
old-fashioned walk.   Homework.   Paris wakes up and
smiles.   Only for Americans.   Just one way to say I
love you.   You can have him.   The policeman's ball.   Falling
out of love can be fun.   "Give me your tired, your poor."

Mr. President.   OC
Columbia KOL 5870/KOS 2270 (1962)
Cast: Nanette Fabray, Jack Haskell.
Credits: Music and lyrics, Irving Berlin; book, Howard
Lindsay and Russel Crouse.
Songs: Is he the only man in the world?   Empty pockets
filled with love.   Glad to be home.   The first lady.   Don't
be afraid of romance.   I'm gonna get him.   In our hide-
away.   Laugh it up.   I've got to be around.   Let's go back
to the waltz.   This is a great country.

The Most happy fella.   OC
Columbia 03L-240 (1956);   Columbia OL 5118 (1956);   Co-
lumbia OS 2330 (1963)
Cast: Robert Weede.
Credits: Music, lyrics, and book, Frank Loesser; based on
Sidney Howard's They knew what they wanted.
Songs: Ooh, my feet.   Somebody somewhere.   The most
happy fella.   Standing on the corner.   Joey, Joey, Joey.
Rosabella.   Abbondanza.   Sposalizio.   Don't cry.   Happy
to make your acquaintance.   Big "D".   How beautiful the
days.   Warm all over.   I like everybody.   My heart is
so full of you.   Mama, mama.   Song of a summer night.
I made a first.

The Most happy fella.   OC
Angel 35887/S35887 (1961)
Cast: Original London cast.
Credits: Music, lyrics and book, Frank Loesser; based on
Sidney Howard's They knew what they wanted.

The Music man.   OC
Capitol WAO/SWAO 990 (1958)
Cast: Robert Preston, Barbara Cook, David Burns, Pert
Kelton.

Credits: Music, book, and lyrics, Meredith Willson.
Songs: Iowa stubborn.   Trouble.   Piano lesson.   Goodnight
 my someone.   Seventy-six trombones.   Sincere.   The sadder but wiser girl.   Pick-a-little, talk-a-little, and goodnight ladies.   Marian, the librarian.   My white knight.
 Wells Fargo wagon.   It's you.   Shipoopi.   Lida Rose and
 will I ever tell you?   Gary, Indiana.   Till there was you.

The Music man.   OC
Stanyan SR   10039 (1968)
Cast: Van Johnson;   original London cast.
Credits: Music, book, and lyrics, Meredith Willson.

My fair lady.
Columbia OL   5090 (1956)
Cast: Rex Harrison, Julie Andrews.
Credits: Music, Frederick Loewe;   book and lyrics, Alan
 Jay Lerner.
Songs: Why can't the English?   Wouldn't it be loverly?
 With a little bit of luck.   I'm an ordinary man.   Just
 you wait.   The rain in Spain.   I could have danced all
 night.   On the street where you live.   You did it.   Show
 me.   Get me to the church on time.   A hymn to him.
 Without you.   I've grown accustomed to her face.

My fair lady.
Columbia OS   2015 (1959)
Recorded February 1, 1959.
Cast: Rex Harrison, Julie Andrews.
Credits: Music, Frederick Loewe;   book and lyrics, Alan
 Jay Lerner.

My fair lady.
RCA Victor LPM/LSP   2274 (1960)
Cast: Jan Peerce, Robert Merrill, Jane Powell, Phil Harris.
Credits: Music, Frederick Loewe;   book and lyrics, Alan
 Jay Lerner.

My fair lady.   OC
Columbia PS   34197 (1976)
Cast: Ian Richardson, Christine Andreas, George Roie,
 Robert Coote.
Credits: Music, Frederick Loewe;   book and lyrics, Alan
 Jay Lerner.

The Nervous set.
Columbia OL 5430/OS   2018 (1959)
Cast: Richard Hayes, Tani Seitz.
Credits: Music, Thomas J. Wolf;   lyrics, Fran Landesman;
  book, Jay Landesman and Theodore J. Flicker.

New faces of 1952.   OC
RCA Victor LOC   1008 (1952);   RCA CBM   1-2206 (1977)
Cast: Ronny Graham, Alice Ghostley, Paul Lynde, Robert
  Clary, Eartha Kitt.
Songs: Lucky Pierre.   Boston beguine.   Love is a simple
  thing.   Nanty puts her hair up.   Guess who I saw today.
  Bal petit bal.   Three for the road.   Penny candy.   Don't
  fall asleep.   I'm in love with Miss Logan.   Monotonous.
  Time for tea.   Lizzie Borden.   He takes me off his in-
  come tax.

New faces of 1968.   OC
Warner Bros.   BS   2551 (1968)

New girl in town.   OC
RCA Victor LOC   1027 (1957);   RCA Victor LSO   1027 (1958);
  RCA Victor LSO   1106 (1965)
Cast: Gwen Verdon, Thelma Ritter.
Credits: Music and lyrics, Bob Merrill.
Songs: It's good to be alive.   If that was love.   Sunshine
  girl.   Ven I valse.   Did you close your eyes?   Look at
  'er.   Flings.

The New moon.
Capitol W/SW   1966 (1963);   Angel   S-37320 (1978)
Cast: Gordon MacRae, Dorothy Kirsten.
Credits: Music, Sigmund Romberg;   lyrics, Oscar Hammerstein II;   book, Oscar Hammerstein II, Laurence Schwab,
  and Frank Mandel.
Songs: Marianne.   The girl on the prow.   Softly, as in a
  morning sunrise.   One kiss.   Stouthearted men.   Wanting
  you.   Lover, come back to me.   Try her out at dances.

The New moon.
Monmouth Evergreen MES   7051 (1973)
Cast: Evelyn Laye.
Credits: Music, Sigmund Romberg;   lyrics, Oscar Hammer-
  stein II;   book, Oscar Hammerstein II, Laurence Schwab,
  and Frank Mandel.
Songs: I was a stranger in Paris.   Softly as in a morning
  sunrise.   Wanting you.   One kiss.   Stouthearted men.
  Lover, come back to me.

No, no, Nanette.   OC
Columbia S30563 (1971)
Cast: Ruby Keeler, Jack Gilford, Bobby Van, Helen Gallagher, Susan Watson, Patsy Kelly.
Credits: Music, Vincent Youmans; lyrics, Irving Caesar
   and Otto Harbach; book, Otto Harbach and Frank Mandel.
Songs: Too many rings around Rosie.   I've confessed to the
   breeze.   Call of the sea.   I want to be happy.   You can
   dance with any girl.   No, no, Nanette.   Tea for two.
   Telephone girlie.   "Where-has-my-hubby-gone."   Waiting
   for you.   Take a little one-step.

No, no, Nanette.   OC
Stanyan SR 10035 (1972)
Cast: Binnie Hale; original London cast.
Credits: Music, Vincent Youmans; lyrics, Irving Caesar
   and Otto Harbach; book, Otto Harbach and Frank Mandel.

No strings.   OC
Capitol O/SO 1695 (1962)
Credits: Music and lyrics, Richard Rodgers.

Now is the time for all good men.   OC
Columbia OL 6730/OS 3130 (1967)
Credits: Music, Nancy Ford; book and lyrics, Gretchen
   Cryer.

Nymph errant.
Monmouth Evergreen MES 7043 (1972)
Cast: Gertrude Lawrence.
Credits: Music and lyrics, Cole Porter; book, Romney
   Brent.
Songs: Experiment.   It's bad for me.   How could we be
   wrong?

Of thee I sing!   OC
Capitol S 350 (1952);   Capitol T 11651 (1977)
Cast: Jack Carson, Paul Hartman.
Credits: Music, George Gershwin; lyrics, Ira Gershwin;
   book, George S. Kaufman and Morrie Ryskind.
Songs: Wintergreen for President!   Who is the lucky girl
   to be?   The dimple on my knee.   Because, because, because.   Some girls can bake a pie.   Love is sweeping the
   country.   Of thee I sing!   Here's a kiss for Cinderella.

I was the most beautiful blossom. Hello, good morning.
Mine. Who cares. Illegitimate daughter of an illegitimate
son of an illegitimate nephew of Napoleon! Jilted. I'm
about to be a mother.

Oh! Calcutta! OC
RCA International INTS 1178 (1970)
Cast: Original Australian cast.
Songs: Oh! Calcutta! Coming together, coming together.
Sincere replies. Dick and Jane. Clarence and Mildred.
Exchanges of information. I like the look. Jack and
Jill. Green pants. Too much too soon.

Oh captain. OC
Columbia OL 5280 (1958); CSP AOS 2002 (1973)
Cast: Tony Randall, Jacquelyn McKeever, Edward Platt.
Credits: Music and lyrics, Jay Livingston and Ray Evans;
book, Al Morgan and José Ferrer.
Songs: A very proper town. Life does a man a favor.
Captain Henry St. James. Three paradises. Surprise.
Hey, madame. Femininity. It's never quite the same.
We're not children. Give it all you got. Love is hell.
Keep it simple. The morning music of Montmartre.
You don't know him. I've been there and I'm back.
Double standard. You're so right for me. All the time.

Oh captain.
MGM Records E 3687 (1958)
Cast: José Ferrer, Rosemary Clooney.
Credits: Music and lyrics, Jay Livingston and Ray Evans;
book, Al Morgan and José Ferrer.

Oh Coward! OC
Bell 9001 (1973)
Cast: Barbara Cason, Roderick Cook, Jamie Ross.
Credits: Words and music, Noël Coward.

Oh, Kay!
Columbia CL 1050 (1957); Columbia OL 7050/OS 2550
(1964); CSP ACL 1050 (1973)
Cast: Barbara Ruick, Jack Cassidy, Allen Case, Roger
White.
Credits: Music, George Gershwin; lyrics, Ira Gershwin;
book, Guy Bolton and P. G. Wodehouse.
Songs: The woman's touch. Don't ask. Dear little girl.
Maybe. Clap yo' hands. Bride and groom. Do, do, do.
Someone to watch over me. Fidgety feet. Heaven on
earth. Oh, Kay!

Oh, Kay!
Monmouth Evergreen MES   7043 (1972)
Cast: Gertrude Lawrence.
Credits: Music, George Gershwin;   lyrics, Ira Gershwin;
  book, Guy Bolton and P. G. Wodehouse.
Songs: Someone to watch over me.   Do, do, do.   Maybe.

Oh say can you see?
RCA Victor LSP   4719 (1972)
Cast: Charles Linton.
Credits: Music, Pierre Nolès and Charles Linton.
Songs: Uncle Sam über alles.   Rules.   Liberated man.
  Diplomacy game.   Centuries pass.   Eternity never changes.
  Is it all America's fault?   New Salvation Army.   Get back
  to love.   God.   Learn how to love to live.   Everybody's
  dream.   Oh say can you see?

Oh, what a lovely war.   OC
London OS   25906 (1965)
Cast: Charles Chilton;   original London cast.
Credits: Music and lyrics, Theatre Workshop, London.
Songs: Row, row, row.   Your king and country want you.
  Belgium put the kibosh on the kaiser.   Are we downhearted.
  Hold your hand out you naughty boy.   I'll make a man of
  you.   Pack up your troubles.   Hitchy koo.   Heilige Nacht.
  Christmas day in the cookhouse.   Good byee.   Oh, it's a
  lovely war.   Gassed last night.   There's a long long trail.
  Hush, here comes a whizbang.   They were only playing
  leapfrog.   I wore a tunic.   Joe Soap's army.   When this
  lousy war is over.   Wash me in the water.   I want to go
  home.   The bells of hell.   Keep the home fires burning.
  Le chanson de Craonne.   I don't want to be a soldier.
  They didn't believe me.

Oklahoma.   OC
Decca DL   9017 (1958);   MCA Records MCA   2030 (1970)
Cast: Alfred Drake, Joan Roberts, Celeste Holm, Howard
  Da Silva, Lee Dixon.
Credits: Music, Richard Rodgers;   book and lyrics, Oscar
  Hammerstein II.
Songs: Oh, what a beautiful mornin'.   The surrey with the
  fringe on top.   Kansas City.   I cain't say no.   Many a
  new day.   People will say we're in love.   Poor Jud is
  daid.   Out of my dreams.   All er nothin!

Oklahoma.
Epic LN 3678/BN   562 (1960)
Cast: Stuart Foster, Lois Hunt.

Credits: Music, Richard Rodgers;   book and lyrics, Oscar
    Hammerstein II.

Oklahoma.
Columbia CL   828 (1956);   Columbia CS   8739 (1963);
    Harmony   11164 (1966)
Cast: Nelson Eddy, Kaye Ballard.
Credits: Music, Richard Rodgers;   book and lyrics, Oscar
    Hammerstein II.

Oklahoma.
Columbia OL 8010/OS   2610 (1964)
Cast: John Raitt, Florence Henderson, Phyllis Newman.
Credits: Music, Richard Rodgers;   book and lyrics, Oscar
    Hammerstein II.
Songs: Oh, what a beautiful mornin'.   The surrey with the
    fringe on top.   Kansas City.   I cain't say no.   Many a
    new day.   People will say we're in love.   Pore Jud.
    Lonely room.   Out of my dreams.   The farmer and the
    cowman.   All er nothin!   Oklahoma.

Oliver!
Capitol T/ST   1784 (1962)
Cast: Violet Carson, Stanley Holloway, Alma Cogan.
Credits: Music, lyrics, and book, Lionel Bart.
Songs: Food, glorious food.   Oliver.   I shall scream.   Boy
    for sale.   Where is love?   Consider yourself.   Pick a
    pocket or two.   It's a fine life.   Be back soon.   I'd do any-
    thing.   Oom-pah-pah.   My name.   As long as he needs me.
    Who will buy this wonderful morning?   Reviewing the situation.

Oliver!   OC
RCA Victor LOCD/LSOD   2004 (1962)
Cast: Clive Revill, Gloria Brown, Bruce Prochnik.
Credits: Music, lyrics, and book, Lionel Bart.
Songs: Food, glorious food.   Oliver.   I shall scream.   Boy
    for sale.   Where is love?   Consider yourself.   You've got
    to pick a pocket or two.   It's a fine life.   Be back soon.
    Oom-pah-pah.   My name.   As long as he needs me.   Who
    will buy?   Reviewing the situation.   I'd do anything.

On a clear day you can see forever.   OC
RCA Victor LOCD/LSOD   2006 (1965)
Cast: Barbara Harris, John Cullum.
Credits: Music, Burton Lane; book/lyrics, Alan Jay Lerner.
Songs: Hurry!   It's a lovely up here!   Tosy and cosh.   On
    a clear day.   On the S. S. Bernard Cohn.   Don't tamper
    with my sister.   She wasn't you.   Melinda.   When I'm

being born again.   What did I have that I don't have?
Wait till we're sixty-five.   Come back to me.

On the town.   OC
Columbia OL 5540/OS 2028 (1961);   Columbia S   31005 (1970)
Cast: Nancy Walker, Betty Comden, Adolph Green, John
   Reardon.
Credits: Music, Leonard Bernstein; lyrics, Betty Comden
   and Adolph Green.
Songs: New York, New York.   Come up to my place.   Car-
   ried away. Lonely town.   Carnegie Hall.   I can cook too.
   Lucky to be me.   So long baby.   I'm blue.   Ya got me.
   Some other time.

On the Twentieth Century.   OC
Columbia PS   35330 (1978)
Cast: John Cullum, Madeleine Kahn, Imogene Coca.
Credits: Music, Cy Coleman; book and lyrics, Betty Com-
   den and Adolph Green.
Songs: Stranded again.   On the Twentieth Century.   I rise
   again. Veronique. Together. Never. Our private world.
   Repent.   Mine.   I've got it all.   Five zeros.   Sextet.
   She's a nut.   Babette.   The legacy.   Lily, Oscar.   Life
   is like a train.

On your toes.   OC
Columbia ML 4645 (1954);   Columbia CL 837 (1956);   Columbia OL 7090/OS 2590 (1964)
Cast: Portia Nelson, Jack Cassidy.
Credits: Music, Richard Rodgers; lyrics, Lorenz Hart;
   book, Richard Rodgers, Lorenz Hart and George Abbott.
Songs: It's gotta be love.   Two a day for Keith.   There's
   a small hotel.   The heart is quicker than the eye.   Quiet
   night. Questions and answers.   On your toes.   Too good
   for the average man.   Glad to be unhappy.

On your toes.
Monmouth Evergreen MES 7049 (1972)
Cast: Jack Whiting.
Credits: Music, Richard Rodgers; lyrics, Lorenz Hart;
   book, Richard Rodgers, Lorenz Hart, and George Abbott.
Songs: On your toes.   There's a small hotel.

On your toes.   OC
Decca DL 9015 (1954)
Cast: Vera Zorina, Bobby Van.
Credits: Music, Richard Rodgers; lyrics, Lorenz Hart;
   book, Richard Rodgers, Lorenz Hart, and George Abbott.

Once upon a mattress.
Kapp KRS 5507 (1967); MCA Records MCA 2079 (1973)
Cast: Carol Burnett.
Credits: Music, Mary Rodgers; lyrics, Marshall Barer.
Songs: Many moons ago. An opening for a princess. In
a little while. Shy. Sensitivity. The swamps of home.
Normandy. Song of love. Spanish panic. Happily ever
after. Man to man talk. Very soft shoes. Yesterday
I loved you.

110 in the shade. OC
RCA Victor LOC/LSO 1085 (1963)
Credits: Music, Harvey Schmidt; lyrics, Tom Jones.

Oops! OC
Wave 0001 (1973)
Cast: Doug Chamberlain, Keith Hampshire, Connie Martin;
original Toronto cast.
Credits: Music and lyrics, David Warrack.
Songs: Lookin' at the world tonight. The sample. Save
the streetcar. It's not the same. Oops! Deflation.
Listen. Where are you going? It's a sin. We'll be
free. I fergive ya fer bein' whatcha are. Let's get a
divorce. Brand new me. Once I knew a girl like you.
That rosy future. We gotta try.

Our love letter.
Capitol T/ST 1941 (1963)
Cast: Judy Garland, John Ireland.
Credits: Music and lyrics, Gordon Jenkins.

Out of this world. OC
Columbia OL 4390 (1953); CSP CML 4390 (1973)
Cast: Charlotte Greenwood.
Credits: Music and lyrics, Cole Porter; book, Dwight Taylor and Reginald Lawrence.
Songs: I Jupiter, I rex. Use your imagination. Hail, hail,
hail. I got beauty. Where, oh where. I am loved. They
couldn't compare to you. What do you think about men. I
sleep easier now. Climb up the mountain. No lover for
me. Cherry pies ought to be you. Hark to the song of
the night. Nobody's chasing me.

Over here. OC
Columbia KS 32961 (1974)
Cast: Andrews Sister.
Credits: Music and lyrics, Richard M. Sherman and Robert
B. Sherman.

Pacific 1860. OC
Show Biz Records   5602 (1976)
Cast: Noël Coward, Mary Martin, Graham Payn;   original
   London cast.
Credits: Music and lyrics, Noël Coward.
Songs: Family grace. If I were a man. Dear Madame Salvador.
   My horse has cast a shoe. I wish I wasn't quite such a big
   girl. Samolan song. Bright was the day. Invitation to the
   waltz. His excellency regrets. The party's going with a
   swing. Birthday toast. Make way for their excellencies.
   Fumfumbolo. One two three. This is a night for lovers. I
   never knew. This is a changing world. Come back to the is-
   land. Gipsy melody. This is the night. Mother's lament.
   Pretty little bridesmaids. I saw no shadow. Wedding toast.
   Uncle Harry.

Pacific overtures. OC
RCA Red Seal ARL 1-1367 (1976)
Cast: Mako, Soon-Tech Oh.
Credits: Music and lyrics, Stephen Sondheim; book, John
   Weidman.
Songs: The advantages of floating in the middle of the sea.
   There is no other way. Four black dragons. Chrysanthemum
   tea. Poems. Welcome to Kanagawa. Someone in a tree.
   Please hello. A bowler hat. Pretty lady. Next.

Paint your wagon. OC
RCA Victor LOC 1006 (1952); RCA Victor LSO 1006 (e) (1965)
Cast: Olga San Juan, Tony Bavaar, Robert Penn, James Bar-
   ton.
Credits: Music, Frederick Loewe; book and lyrics, Alan Jay
   Lerner.
Songs: I'm on my way. Rumson. What's goin' on here? I talk
   to the trees. They call the wind Maria. I still see Elisa.
   How can I wait? In between. Whoop-ti-ay! Carino mio.
   There's a coach comin' in. Hand me down that can o' beans.
   Another autumn. All for him. Wand'rin' star.

Paint your wagon.
RCA Victor LPM/LSP 2274 (1960)
Cast: Jan Peerce, Robert Merrill, Jane Powell, Phil Harris.
Credits: Music, Frederick Loewe; book and lyrics, Alan Jay
   Lerner.

The Pajama game.
Columbia OL 4840 (1954); Columbia S 32606 (1973)
Cast: John Raitt, Janis Paige, Eddie Foy, Jr.

Credits: Music and lyrics, Richard Adler and Jerry Ross;
    book, George Abbott and Richard Bissell;   based on the
    novel $7\frac{1}{2}$ cents, by Richard Bissell.
Songs: The pajama game.   Racing with the clock.   I'm not
    at all in love.   I'll never be jealous again.   Hey there.
    Once-a-year day.   Small talk.   There once was a man.
    Steam heat.   Hernando's hideaway. $7\frac{1}{2}$ cents.

Pal Joey.   OC
Columbia OL   4364 (1952);   CSP COL   4364 (1973)
Cast: Vivienne Segal, Harold Lang.
Credits: Music, Richard Rodgers;   lyrics, Lorenz Hart;
    book, John O'Hara.
Songs: You mustn't kick it around.   I could write a book.
    That terrific rainbow.   What is a man?   Happy hunting
    horn.   Bewitched.   What do I care for a dame.   Zip.
    Plant you now, dig you later.   In our little den of iniquity.
    Do it the hard way.   Take him.

Parade.   OC
Kapp KDL   7005 (1960)
Cast: Dody Goodman.
Credits: Music and lyrics, Jerry Herman.

A Party.   OC
Stet Records S2L   5177 (1977)
Cast: Betty Comden, Adolph Green
Credits: Lyrics, Betty Comden and Adolph Green.
Songs: I said good morning.   The Reader's digest.   The
    screen writers.   The Banshee sisters.   The Baroness
    Bazooka.   New York, New York.   Lonely town.   Lucky
    to be me.   Some other time.   Carried away.   100 easy
    ways to lose a man.   Ohio.   The wrong note rag.   Cap-
    ital gains.   If.   Catch our act at the Met.   The French
    lesson.   The lost word.   Captain Hook's waltz.   Never
    never land.   Mysterious lady.   Simplified language.   In-
    spiration.   Just in time.   Make someone happy.   The
    party's over.

Peter Pan.   OC
Columbia OL   4312 (1950);   CSP AOL   4312 (1973)
Cast: Jean Arthur, Boris Karloff.
Credits: Music and lyrics, Leonard Bernstein.
Songs: Who am I?   Build my house.   Peter, Peter.   The
    pirate song.   The plank.

Peter Pan.   OC
RCA Victor LOC   1019 (1954)
Cast: Mary Martin, Cyril Ritchard.
Credits: Music, Mark Charlap;   lyrics, Carolyn Leigh;
    based on the play by Sir James M. Barrie.
Songs: Tender shepherd.   I've gotta crow.   Never, never
    land.   I'm flying.   Pirate song.   Hook's tango.   Indians.
    Wendy.   Tarantella.   I won't grow up.   Oh my mysterious
    lady.   Ugg-a-wugg.   Distant melody.   Hook's waltz.

Pins and needles.
Columbia OL 5810/OS   2210 (1962)
Credits: Music and lyrics, Harold Rome.

Pipe dream.   OC
RCA Victor LOC/LSO   1097 (1965)
Credits: Music, Richard Rodgers;   lyrics, Oscar Hammer-
    stein II.
Songs: Everybody's got a home but me.   All at once you
    love her.   The man I used to be.   Sweet Thursday.   Think.
    A lopsided bus.   The happiest house on the block.

Pippin.   OC
Motown   M760L (1972)
Cast: Eric Berry, Jill Clayburgh, Leland Palmer, Irene
    Ryan, Ben Vereen, John Rubinstein.
Credits: Music and lyrics, Stephen Schwartz.
Songs: Magic to do.   Corner of the sky.   War is a science.
    Glory.   Simple joys.   No time at all.   With you.   Spread
    a little sunshine.   Morning glow.   On the right track.
    Kind of woman.   Extraordinary.   Love song.   I guess I'll
    miss the man.

Plain and fancy.   OC
Capitol S   603 (1955);   Capitol DW   603 (1969)
Cast: Richard Derr, Shirl Conway.
Credits: Music, Albert Martin Hague;   lyrics, Arnold B.
    Horwitt;   book, Joseph Stein and Will Glickman.

Porgy and Bess.   OC
Decca DL   9024 (1955);   MCA Records MCA   2035 (1973)
Cast: Anne Brown, Todd Duncan.
Credits: Music, George Gershwin;   lyrics, Du Bose Hey-
    ward and Ira Gershwin;   based on Porgy, by Du Bose
    Heyward.
Songs: Summertime.   A woman is a sometime thing.   My
    man's gone now.   It take a long pull to get there.   I got

plenty of nuttin! Buzzard song. Bess, you is my woman.
It ain't necessarily so. What you want wid Bess? I loves
you Porgy. There's a boat dat's leavin' soon for New York.
Porgy's lament.

Les Poupées de Paris. OC
RCA Victor LOC/LSO 1090 (1964)
Cast: Pearl Bailey, Milton Berle, Cyd Charisse, Anne
 Fargé, Gene Kelly, Liberace, Jane Mansfield, Tony Mar-
 tin, Phil Silvers, Loretta Young, Edie Adams.
Credits: Music, James Van Heusen; lyrics, Sammy Cahn.

Primrose. OC
Monmouth Evergreen MES 7071 (1974)
Cast: Leslie Henson; original London cast.
Credits: Music, George Gershwin; lyrics, Desmond Carter
 and Ira Gershwin; book, George Grossmith and Guy Bolton.
Songs: This is the life for a man. When Toby is out of
 town. Some far away someone. The Mophams. Berke-
 ley Square and Kew. Boy wanted. Mary, Queen of Scots.
 Wait a bit, Susie. Naughty baby. That new fangled mother
 of mine. I make hay when the moon shines.

Privates on parade. OC
EMI EMC 3233 (1978)
Cast: Original London cast.
Credits: Music, Denis King; lyrics, Peter Nichols; based
 on Privates on parade, by Peter Nichols.
Songs: SADUSEA. The movie to end them all. The little
 things we used to do. Black velvet. Better far than sit-
 ting this life out. The prince of peace. Could you please
 inform us? Privates on parade. The Latin American way.
 Sunnyside lane. Play off.

Promenade. OC
RCA Victor LSO 1161 (1969)
Cast: Sandra Schaeffer, Ty McConnell, Gilbert Price.
Credits: Music, Al Carmines; book and lyrics, Maria
 Irene Fornes.
Songs: Unrequited love. The cigarette song. A flower.
 Isn't that clear? Two little angels. Four. Chicken is
 he. The passing of time. Crown me. Capricious and
 fickle. The moment has passed. Little fool. The clothes
 make the man. A poor man. Listen, I feel. I saw a
 man. All is well in the city.

Promises, promises. OC
United Artists UAS 9902 (1968)
Cast: Jerry Orbach, Jill O'Hara, Edward Winter.
Credits: Music, Burt Bacharach; lyrics, Hal David.
Songs: Half as big as life. Upstairs. You'll think of some-
   one. Our little secret. She likes basketball. Knowing
   when to leave. Wanting things. Turkey lurkey time. A
   fact can be a beautiful thing. Grapes of Roth. Whoever
   you are. Where can you take a girl? Christmas day.
   A young pretty girl like you. I'll never fall in love again.
   Promises, promises.

Purlie. OC
Ampex Records A 40101 (1970)
Cast: Melba Moore, Cleavon Little.
Credits: Music, Gary Geld.
Songs: Skinnin' a cat. Purlie. The harder they fall. The
   barrels of war. The unborn love. Big fish, little fish.
   God's alive, I got love. Great white father. Down home.
   First thing Monday mornin'. He can do it. The world
   is comin' to a start. Walk him up the stairs.

Raisin. OC
Columbia KS 32754 (1973)
Cast: Virginia Capers, Joe Morton, Ernestine Jackson.
Credits: Music, Judd Woldin; lyrics, Robert Brittan; book,
   Robert Nemiroff and Charlotte Zaltzberg; based on A rai-
   sin in the sun, by Lorraine Hansberry.
Songs: Man say. Whose little angry man. Runnin' to meet
   the man. A whole lotta sunlight. Alaiyo. Sweet time.
   You done right. He come down this morning. It's a deal.
   Sidewalk tree. Not anymore. Measure the valleys.

The Real ambassadors. OC
Columbia OL 5850/OS 2250 (1962)
Cast: Louis Armstrong, Dave Brubeck, Iola Brubeck.
Credits: Music, Dave Brubeck; book and lyrics, Iola Bru-
   beck.

Redhead. OC
RCA Victor LOC 1048 (1959); RCA Victor LOC/LSO 1104
   (1965)
Cast: Gwen Verdon, Richard Kiley.
Credits: Music, Albert Martin Hague; lyrics, Dorothy Fields

book, Herbert and Dorothy Fields, Sidney Sheldon, and
David Shaw.
Songs: The Simpson sisters. The right finger of my left
hand. Just for once. I feel merely marvelous. The
Uncle Sam rag. Erbie Fitch's twitch. She's not enough
woman for me. Behave yourself. Look who's in love.
The girl is just enough woman for me. Two faces in the
dark. I'm back in circulation. We loves ya, Jimey.
I'll try.

Rex. OC
RCA Records ABL 1-1683 (1976)
Cast: Nicol Williamson, Penny Fuller.
Credits: Music, Richard Rodgers; lyrics, Sheldon Harnick;
book, Sherman Yellen.
Songs: No song more pleasing. At the field of cloth of
gold. Where is my son? As once I loved you. The
chase. Away from you. Elizabeth. Why? So much
you loved me. Christmas at Hampton Court. The wee
golden warrior. From afar. In time. Te Deum.

Rio Rita.
Monmouth Evergreen MES 7058 (1972)
Cast: Edith Day.
Credits: Music, Harry Tierney; lyrics, Joseph McCarthy;
book, Guy Bolton and Fred Thompson.
Songs: Rio Rita. Sweetheart, we need each other. The
song of the rangers. Following the sun around. The
best little lover in town. You're always in my arms.
If you're in love, you'll waltz. Kinkajou.

The Roar of the greasepaint. OC
RCA Victor LOC/LSO 1109 (1965)
Cast: Anthony Newley, Cyril Ritchard.
Credits: Music, lyrics, and book, Anthony Newley and Les-
lie Bricusse.
Songs: The beautiful land. A wonderful day like today. It
isn't enough. Things to remember. Put it in the book.
Will all due respect. This dream. Where would you be
without me? My first love song. Look at that face. The
joker. Who can I turn to? That's what it is to be young.
What a man! Feeling good. Nothing can stop me now!
My way. Sweet beginning.

Roberta. OC
Columbia CL 841 (1956); Columbia OL 7030/OS 2530 (1964);

CSP COS   2530 (1973)
Cast: Joan Roberts, Jack Cassidy, Kaye Ballard, Portia Nelson.
Credits: Music, Jerome Kern; lyrics, Otto Harbach, Dorothy Fields, and Jimmy McHugh; book, Otto Harbach; based on Gowns by Roberta, by Alice Duer Miller.
Songs: I won't dance. You're devastating. Yesterdays. The touch of your hand. I'll be hard to handle. Smoke gets in your eyes. Lovely to look at. Let's begin.

Roberta.
Capitol T-351 (1958)
Cast: Gordon MacRae, Lucille Norman.
Credits: Music, Jerome Kern; lyrics, Otto Harbach, Dorothy Fields, and Jimmy McHugh; book, Otto Harbach; based on Gowns by Roberta, by Alice Duer Miller.

Rose Marie.
RCA Victor LOP/LSO   1001 (1959)
Cast: Julie Andrews, Giorgio Tozzi.
Credits: Music, Rudolf Friml and Herbert Stothart; book and lyrics, Otto Harbach and Oscar Hammerstein II.
Songs: Rose Marie. The Indian love call. The song of the mounties. The door of my dreams. Totem tom tom.

The Rothschilds. OC
Columbia S   30337 (1970)
Cast: Paul Hecht, Keene Curtis, Leila Martin, Jill Clayburgh, Hal Linden.
Credits: Music, Jerry Bock; lyrics, Sheldon Harnick; book, Sherman Yellen; based on The Rothschilds, by Frederic Morton.
Songs: Pleasure and privilege. One room. He tossed a coin. Sons. Everything. Rothschild and Sons. Allons. Give England strength. This amazing London town. They say. I'm in love! I'm in love! In my own lifetime. Have you ever seen a prettier little congress? Bonds. The will.

Rugantino. OC
Warner Bros. H/HS   1528 (1964)
Credits: Music, Armando Trovajoli.

Runaways. OC
Columbia JS   35410 (1978)
Cast: Cast of the New York Shakespeare Festival Production.
Credits: Music and lyrics, Elizabeth Swados.

Songs: Where do people go?   Every now and then.   Minne-
    sota strip.   Song of a child prostitute.   Find me a hero.
    The undiscovered son.   No lullabies for Luis.   We are
    not strangers.   The basketball song.   Let me be a kid.
    Revenge song.   Enterprise.   Lullaby from baby to baby.
    Sometimes.   Where are those people who did "Hair"?
    To the dead of family wars.   Lonesome of the road.

Sail away.   OC
Stanyan SR   10027 (1973)
Cast: Elaine Stritch, David Holliday;   original London cast.
Credits: Music, lyrics, and book, Noël Coward.
Songs: Come to me.   Sail away.   Where shall I find him?
    Beatnik love affair.   Later than spring.   Useless useful
    phrases.   The passenger's always right.   You're a long
    way from America.   The customer's always right.   Go
    slow, Johnny.   Something very strange.   Don't turn away
    from love.   Bronxville Darby and Joan.   When you want
    me.   Why do the wrong people travel?

Sail away.   OC
Capitol WAO/SWAO   1643 (1961)
Credits: Music, lyrics, and book, Noël Coward.

Sail away.
Capitol W/SW   1667 (1962)
Cast: Noël Coward.
Credits: Music, lyrics, and book, Noël Coward.

St. Louis woman.   OC
Capitol DW   2742 (1967)
Cast: Pearl Bailey, Ruby Hill, Rex Ingram.
Credits: Music, Harold Arlen;   lyrics, Johnny Mercer;
    book, Arna Bontemps and Countee Cullen.
Songs: Come rain or come shine.   Legalize my name.   Any
    place I hang my hat is home.   Ridin' on the moon.   A
    woman's prerogative.   I had myself a true love.

Salad days.   OC
Oriole MG   20004 (1970)
Cast: Eleanor Drew, John Warner.
Credits: Book and lyrics, Dorothy Reynolds and Julian Slade;
    music, Julian Slade.
Songs: The things that are done by a don.   We said we

wouldn't look back.   Find yourself something to do.   I
sit in the sun.   Oh, look at me.   Hush-hush.   Out of
breath.   Cleopatra.   It's easy to sing.   We're looking
for a piano.   The time of my life.   The saucer song.

Sally.   OC
Monmouth Evergreen MES   7053 (1973)
Cast: Dorothy Dickson, Gregory Stroud, Leslie Henson;
    original London cast.
Credits: Music, Jerome Kern; lyrics, Clifford Grey and
    Buddy DeSylva; book, Guy Bolton.
Songs: You can't keep a good girl down.   Look for the sil-
    ver lining.   Sally.   Wild rose.   The Schnitza-Komisski.
    The Lorelei.   Whip-poor-will.   The church 'round the
    corner.

Salvation.   OC
Capitol SO   337 (1969)
Credits: Music, lyrics, and book, Peter Link and C. C.
    Courtney.

Saratoga.   OC
RCA Victor LOC/LSO   1051 (1959)
Cast: Howard Keel.
Credits: Music, Harold Arlen; lyrics, Johnny Mercer.
Songs: Dog eat dog.   A game of poker.   Goose never be
    a peacock.   Love held lightly.   The man in my life.
    The parks of Paris.   Petticoat high.   You for me.
    Saratoga.

Say, darling.   OC
RCA Victor LOC/LSO   1045 (1958)
Cast: David Wayne, Vivian Blaine, Johnny Desmond.
Credits: Music, Jule Styne; lyrics, Betty Comden and
    Adolph Green.

Scream on someone you love.
Verve V   15056 (1967)
Cast: Jack E. Leonard.
Credits: Music and lyrics, Bob Booker and George Foster.

The Secret life of Walter Mitty.   OC
Columbia OL 6320/OS   2720 (1965); CSP ADS   2720 (1973)
Cast: Marc London, Cathryn Damon, Eugene Roche.
Credits: Music, Leon Carr; lyrics, Earl Schuman; book,
    Joe Manchester; based on The secret life of Walter Mitty,
    by James Thurber.

Songs: The secret life. The Walter Mitty march. Walking
with Peninnah. Drip, drop tapoketa. Aggie. Don't forget. Marriage is for old folks. Willa. Confidence.
Hello, I love you, goodbye. Fan the flame. Two little
pussy cats. Now that I am forty. You're not. Lonely
ones.

Seesaw. OC
Buddah BDC 95006-10C (1973)
Cast: Michele Lee, Ken Howard.
Credits: Music, Cy Coleman; lyrics, Dorothy Fields;
based on Two for the seesaw, by William Gibson.
Songs: Seesaw. My city. Nobody does it like me. In
tune. Spanglish. Welcome to Holiday Inn. You're a
loveable lunatic. He's good for me. Ride out the storm.
Entire act. We've got it. Poor everybody else. Chapter
54, number 1909. It's not where you start.

Seventeen. OC
RCA Red Seal CBM 1-2034 (1976)
Cast: Kenneth Nelson, Ann Crowley.
Credits: Music, Walter Kent; lyrics, Kim Gannon; book,
Sally Benson; based on Seventeen, by Booth Tarkington.
Songs: Weatherbee's drug store. This was just another
day. Things are gonna hum this summer. How do you
do, Miss Pratt. Summertime is summertime. Reciproc-
ity. Ode to Lola. A headache and a heartache. Ooh,
ooh, ooh, what you do to me. The Hoosier way. I
could get married today. After all it's spring. If we
could only stop the old town clock.

1776. OC
Columbia BOS 3310 (1969)
Cast: William Daniels, Paul Hecht, Clifford David, Roy
Poole, Rex Everhart.
Credits: Music and lyrics, Sherman Edwards; book, Peter
Stone.
Songs: Sit down, John. Piddle, twiddle and resolve. The
Lees of old Virginia. But, Mr. Adams. Yours, yours,
yours. He plays the violin. Cool, cool, considerate men.
Momma look sharp. The egg. Molasses to rum. Is
anybody there?

70, girls 70. OC
Columbia S 30589 (1971)
Cast: Mildred Natwick, Hans Conried, Lillian Roth.
Credits: Music, John Kander; lyrics, Fred Ebb.

Shades.
Mark MC   8634 (1976)
Credits: Music and lyrics, Laura Byers Samuelson.

She loves me.   OC
MGM Records E   4118 OC (1963)
Cast: Barbara Cook, Daniel Massey, Barbara Baxley.
Credits: Music, Jerry Bock; lyrics, Sheldon Harnick;
    book, Joe Masteroff.

Shenandoah.   OC
RCA Red Seal ARL   1-1019 (1975)
Cast: John Cullum.
Credits: Music, Gary Geld; lyrics, Peter Udell.
Songs: Raise the flag of Dixie.   I've heard it all before.
    Why am I me?   Next to lovin' (I like fightin').   Over
    the hill.   The pickers are comin'.   Meditation.   We make
    a beautiful pair.   Violets and silverbells.   It's a boy.
    Papa's gonna make it alright.   Freedom.   The only home
    I know.   Pass the cross to me.

Show biz.
RCA Victor LOC   1011 (1955)
Cast: Recordings of various entertainers with narration by
    George Jessel.
Credits: Music and lyrics, George Abel and Joe Laurie Jr.;
    based on Show biz, by George Abel.
Contents: When vaudeville was king, 1904 to 1920.   The
    roaring twenties, 1920 to 1929.   When Wall Street laid
    an egg, 1929 to 1940.   From TV to 3-D, 1940 to present.

Show boat.
RCA Victrola AVM   1-1741 (1976)
Cast: Patrice Munsel, Helen Morgan, Robert Merrill, Paul
    Robeson.
Credits: Music, Jerome Kern; book and lyrics, Oscar
    Hammerstein II; based on Show boat, by Edna Ferber.

Show boat.   OC
RCA Victor LOC/LSO   1126 (1966)
Cast: Barbara Cook, Constance Towers, Stephen Douglass,
    David Wayne, William Warfield.
Credits: Music, Jerome Kern; book and lyrics, Oscar
    Hammerstein II; based on Show boat, by Edna Ferber.
Songs: Cotton blossom.   Make believe.   Ol' man river.
    Can't help lovin' dat man.   Life upon the wicked stage.
    You are love.   At the Chicago world's fair.   Why do I
    love you?   Bill.   Good bye my lady love.   After the ball.

Show boat. OC
Stanyan 2 SR 10048 (1972)
Cast: Andre Jobin, Cleo Laine, Thomas Carey, Kenneth
  Nelson, Derek Royle, Lorna Dallas; original London cast.
Credits: Music, Jerome Kern; book and lyrics, Oscar
  Hammerstein II; based on Show boat, by Edna Ferber.
Songs: Cotton blossom. Where's the mate for me? Make
  believe. Can't help lovin' dat man. I might fall back
  on you. Ol' man river. How'd you like to spoon with
  me? You are love. I still suits me. Queenie's bally-
  hoo. The wedding. Nobody else but me. Till good luck
  comes my way. Life upon the wicked stage. I have the
  room above her. At the fair. Bill. After the ball.
  Dance away the night. Why do I love you?

Show boat.
Columbia OL 4058 (1950)
Cast: Carol Bruce, Paul Clayton.
Credits: Music, Jerome Kern; book and lyrics, Oscar
  Hammerstein II; based on Show boat, by Edna Ferber.

Show boat.
Columbia OL 5820/OS 2220 (1962)
Cast: John Raitt, Barbara Cook, William Warfield, Anita
  Darian.
Credits: Music, Jerome Kern; book and lyrics, Oscar
  Hammerstein II; based on Show boat, by Edna Ferber.

Show boat.
RCA Victor LM 2008 (1956)
Cast: Patrice Munsel, Risë Stevens, Robert Merrill.
Credits: Music, Jerome Kern; book and lyrics, Oscar
  Hammerstein II; based on Show boat, by Edna Ferber.

Show boat.
CSP AC-55 (1974)
Cast: Helen Morgan, Frank Munn, Emma Albani, James
  Melton, Paul Robeson.
Credits: Music, Jerome Kern; book and lyrics, Oscar
  Hammerstein II; based on Show boat, by Edna Ferber.

Shuffle along. OC
New World Records NW 260 (1976)
Cast: Noble Sissle, Gertrude Saunders.
Credits: Music, Eubie Blake; lyrics, Noble Sissle; book,
  F. E. Miller and Aubrey Lyles.
Songs: Bandana days. I'm just wild about Harry. In honey-

suckle time.   Love will find a way.   Daddy, won't you
please come home.   Baltimore buzz.   Gypsy blues.   I'm
craving for that kind of love.   The fight.   Gee, I'm glad
I'm from Dixie.   Mirandy.   How ya' gonna keep 'em down
on the farm.   On patrol in no man's land.

Side by side by Sondheim.   OC
RCA Red Seal CBL   2-1851 (1976)
Cast: Julia McKenzie, David Kernan, Millicent Martin;
   original London cast.
Credits: Music, Stephen Sondheim.
Songs: Comedy tonight.   Love is in the air.   The little
   things you do together.   You must meet my wife.   Getting
   married today.   I remember.   Can that boy foxtrot.   Too
   many mornings.   Company.   Another hundred people.
Barcelona.   Being alive.   I never do anything twice.
Bring on the girls.   Ah, Paree!   Buddy's blues.   Broadway baby.   You could drive a person crazy.   Everybody
says don't.   There won't be trumpets.   Anyone can whistle.
Send in the clowns.   Pretty lady.   We're gonna be all
right.   A boy like that.   The boy from....   If momma
was married.   Losing my mind.   Could I leave you?   I'm
still here.   Side by side by side.

Silk stockings.   OC
RCA Victor LOC   1016 (1955);   RCA Red Seal CBM   1-2208
   (1977)
Cast: Hildegarde Neff, Don Ameche.
Credits: Music and lyrics, Cole Porter;   book, George S.
   Kaufman, Leveen MacGrath, and Abe Burrows.
Songs: Too bad.   Paris loves lovers.   Stereophonic sound.
   It's a chemical reaction, that's all.   All of you.   Satin
   and silk.   Without love.   Hail Bibinski.   As on through
   the seasons we sail.   Josephine.   Siberia.   Silk stockings.
   The red blues.

Silk stockings.   OC
RCA Victor LOC/LSO   1102 (1965)
Credits: Music and lyrics, Cole Porter;   book, George S.
   Kaufman, Leveen MacGrath, and Abe Burrows.

Simply heaven.   OC
Columbia OL 5240 (1957)
Cast: Claudia McNeil, Melvin Stewart.
Credits: Music, David Martin;   book and lyrics, Langston
   Hughes.

Skyscraper. OC
Capitol SVAS 2422 (1965)
Cast: Julie Harris.
Credits: Music, James Van Heusen; lyrics, Sammy Cahn;
book, Peter Stone.

Song of Norway. OC
Decca DL 9019 (1955); MCA Records MCA 2032 (1973)
Cast: Lawrence Brooks, Helena Bliss, Robert Shafer, Kitty
Carlisle.
Credits: Musical adaptation and lyrics, Robert Wright and
George Forrest; book, Milton Lazarus; based on the
music of Edvard Grieg.
Songs: Hill of dreams. Freddy and his fiddle. Now.
Strange music. Midsummer's eve. March of the troll-
gers. Hymn of betrothal. Bon vivant. Three loves.
Finaletto. I love you. At Christmastime.

Song of Norway.
Angel 35904/S 35904 (1961)
Credits: Musical adaptation and lyrics, Robert Wright and
George Forrest; book, Milton Lazarus; based on the
music of Edvard Grieg.

Song of Norway.
Columbia CL 1328/CS 8135 (1959)
Credits: Musical adaptation and lyrics, Robert Wright and
George Forrest; book, Milton Lazarus; based on the
music of Edvard Grieg.

The Sound of music. OC
Columbia KOL 5450/KOS 2020 (1959); Columbia S 32601
(1973)
Cast: Mary Martin, Theodore Bikel, Patricia Neway, Kurt
Kasznar, Marion Marlowe.
Credits: Music, Richard Rodgers; lyrics, Oscar Hammer-
stein II; book, Howard Lindsay and Russel Crouse; sug-
gested by The Trapp Family Singers, by Maria Augusta
Trapp.
Songs: The sound of music. Maria. My favorite things.
Do-re-mi. Sixteen going on seventeen. The lonely goat-
herd. How can love survive. So long, farewell. Climb
ev'ry mountain. No way to stop it. An ordinary couple.
Processional. Edelweiss.

The Sound of music.
Warner Bros. W/SW 1377 (1960)

Cast: Trapp Family Singers.
Credits: Music, Richard Rodgers; lyrics, Oscar Hammer-
    stein II; book, Howard Lindsay and Russel Crouse; sug-
    gested by The Trapp Family Singers, by Maria Augusta
    Trapp.

South Pacific.   OC
Columbia OL   4180 (1949);   Columbia OS   2040 (1962);   Co-
    lumbia S   32604 (1973)
Cast: Mary Martin, Ezio Pinza, Juanita Hall, William Tab-
    bert.
Credits: Music, Richard Rodgers; lyrics, Oscar Hammer-
    stein II; book, Oscar Hammerstein II and Joshua Logan;
    adapted from Tales of the South Pacific, by James A.
    Michener.
Songs: Dites-moi.   A cockeyed optimist.   Twin soliloquies.
    Some enchanted evening.   Bloody Mary.   There is nothin'
    like a dame.   Bali Ha'i.   I'm gonna wash that man right
    outa my hair.   A wonderful guy.   Younger than spring-
    time.   Happy talk.   Honey Bun.   You've got to be care-
    fully taught.   This nearly was mine.

South Pacific.   OC
Columbia OL 6700/OS   3100 (1967)
Cast: Florence Henderson, Giorgio Tozzi; original cast
    from the Music Theater of Lincoln Center.
Credits: Music, Richard Rodgers; lyrics, Oscar Hammer-
    stein II; book, Oscar Hammerstein II and Joshua Logan;
    adapted from Tales of the South Pacific, by James A.
    Michener.

Starting here, starting now.   OC
RCA Red Seal ABL   1-2360 (1977)
Cast: Loni Ackerman, Margery Cohen, George Lee Andrews.
Credits: Music, David Shire; lyrics, Richard Maltby Jr.
Songs: The word is love.   Starting here, starting now.   A
    little bit off.   I think I may want to remember today.   We
    can talk to each other.   Just across the river.   Cross-
    word puzzle.   Autumn.   I don't remember Christmas.   I
    don't believe it.   Barbara.   Pleased with myself.   Flair.
    Travel.   Watching the big parade go by.   I hear bells.
    What about today?   One step.   Song of me.   Today is the
    first day of the rest of my life.   A new life coming.

Stop the world, I want to get off.   OC
London AM 58001/AMS   88001 (1962)
Cast: Anna Quayle, Jennifer Baker, Susan Baker, Anthony

Newley.
Credits: Music, lyrics, and book, Anthony Newley and Leslie Bricusse.
Songs: The A. B. C. song. I wanna be rich. Typically English. Lumbered. Glorious Russian. Meilinki Meilchick. Gonna build a mountain. Typische Deutsche. Family fugue. Nag!Nag!Nag! Once in a lifetime. All American. Mumbo jumbo. Someone nice like you. What kind of fool am I?

Story theatre. OC
Columbia SG 30415 (1971)
Cast: Hamid Hamilton Camp, Richard Schaal, Richard Libertini, Peter Bonerz, The True Brethren.
Songs: I feel like I'm fixin' to die rag. I'll be your baby tonight. Dear landlord. Here comes the sun.
Stories: Henny Penny. Two crows. The little peasant. The Bremen town musicians. The robber bridegroom. Is he fat. Venus and the cat. The master thief. The fisherman and his wife. The golden goose.

Street scene. OC
Columbia ML 4139 (1947); CSP COL 4139 (1973)
Cast: Anne Jeffreys, Polyna Stoska, Brian Sullivan.
Credits: Music, Kurt Weill; lyrics, Langston Hughes; book, Elmer Rice.
Songs: Moon-faced, starry-eyed. Ain't it awful, the heat? I got a marble and a star. Gossip. When a woman has a baby. Somehow I never could believe. Wrapped in a ribbon and tied in a bow. Lonely house. Wouldn't you like to be on Broadway? What good would the moon be? Remember that I care. Morning. Children's game. A boy like you. We'll go away together. The woman who lived up there. Lullaby. I loved her too. Farewell duet.

The Student prince.
Monmouth Evergreen MES 7054 (1973)
Cast: Harry Welchman, Allan Prior.
Credits: Music, Sigmund Romberg; book and lyrics, Dorothy Donnelly.
Songs: Students' entrance and drinking song. Deep in my heart. Memories. Just we two. Serenade. Golden days.

The Student prince.
RCA Victor LM/LSC 2339 (1960)
Cast: Mario Lanza, Norma Giusti.
Credits: Music, Sigmund Romberg; book and lyrics, Dorothy Donnelly.

Songs: Serenade. Golden days. Drink, drink, drink. Sum-
mertime in Heidelberg. I'll walk with God. Thoughts
will come back to me. Student life. Just we two. Beloved. Gaudeamus igitur. Deep in my heart, dear.

The Student prince.
Capitol P 437 (1953)
Cast: Gordon MacRae, Dorothy Warenskjold.
Credits: Music, Sigmund Romberg; book and lyrics, Dor-
othy Donnelly.

The Student prince.
Capitol W/SW 1841 (1962)
Cast: Dorothy Kirsten, Gorden MacRae.
Credits: Music, Sigmund Romberg; book and lyrics, Dor-
othy Donnelly.

The Student prince.
Columbia CL 826 (1957); Odyssey Y 32367 (1973)
Cast: Dorothy Kirsten, Robert Rounseville.
Credits: Music, Sigmund Romberg; book and lyrics, Dor-
othy Donnelly.

The Student prince.
Columbia OL 5980/OS 2380 (1963)
Cast: Roberta Peters, Jan Peerce, Giorgio Tozzi.
Credits: Music, Sigmund Romberg; book and lyrics,
Dorothy Donnelly.

The Student prince.
Decca DL 8362 (1956)
Cast: Lauritz Melchior.
Credits: Music, Sigmund Romberg; book and lyrics, Dor-
othy Donnelly.

Subways are for sleeping. OC
Columbia KOL 5730/KOS 2130 (1962); CSP AKOS 2130 (1973)
Cast: Sydney Chaplin, Carol Lawrence, Orson Bean, Phyllis
Newman.
Credits: Music, Jule Styne; book and lyrics, Betty Comden and Adolph Green.
Songs: Subways are for sleeping. Girls like me. Subway
directions. Ride through the night. I'm just taking my
time. I was a shoo-in. Who knows what might have
been? Strange duet. Swing your projects. I said it and
I'm glad. Be a Santa. How can you describe a face? I
just can't wait. Comes once in a lifetime. What is this
feeling in the air?

Sugar. OC
United Artists UAS 9905 (1972)
Cast: Elaine Joyce, Robert Morse, Tony Roberts, Cyril
Ritchard.
Credits: Music, Jule Styne; lyrics, Bob Merrill.
Songs: Penniless bums. The beauty that drives men mad.
We could be close. Sun on my face. November song.
Sugar. Hey, why not! Beautiful through and through.
What do you give to a man who's had everything? It's
always love. When you meet a man in Chicago.

Sunny. OC
Stanyan SR 10035 (1972)
Cast: Binnie Hale; original London cast.
Credits: Music, Jerome Kern; lyrics, Otto Harbach and
Oscar Hammerstein II.

Sweet Charity. OC
Columbia KOL 6500/KOS 2900 (1966)
Cast: Gwen Verdon, John McMartin, Helen Gallagher.
Credits: Music, Cy Coleman; lyrics, Dorothy Fields; book,
Neil Simon.
Songs: You should see yourself. Big spender. Charity's
soliloquy. If my friends could see me now. Too many
tomorrows. There's gotta be something better than this.
I'm the bravest individual. The rhythm of life. Baby
dream your dream. Sweet Charity. Where am I going?
I'm a brass band. I love to cry at weddings.

Take me along. OC
RCA Victor LOC/LSO 1050 (1959)
Cast: Jackie Gleason.
Credits: Music and lyrics, Bob Merrill.

Tenderloin. OC
Capitol WAO/SWAO 1492 (1960)
Credits: Music, Jerry Bock; lyrics, Sheldon Harnick.

Three billion millionaires.
United Artists UXL 4 (1964)
Cast: Jack Benny, Carol Burnett, Wally Cox, Bing Crosby,
Sammy Davis Jr. , Judy Garland, Danny Kaye, George
Maharis, Terry Thomas.
Credits: Music, Robert Allen; book and lyrics, Diane Lam-
pert and Peter Farrow.

The Three musketeers.   OC
Monmouth Evergreen MES   7050 (1972)
Cast: Dennis King, Raymond Newell, Adrienne Brune;   orig-
inal London cast.
Credits: Music, Rudolph Friml;   lyrics, Clifford Grey and
P. G. Wodehouse;   book, William A. McGuire;   based on
The three musketeers, by Alexandre Dumas.
Songs: My sword and I.   Ma belle.   Every little while.
Queen of my heart.   Gascony.   Your eyes.   March of
the musketeers.   One kiss.

A Thurber carnival.   OC
Columbia KOL 5500/KOS   2024 (1960)
Cast: Tom Ewell, Peggy Cass, Paul Ford.
Credits: Music, Don Elliott;   words, James Thurber.
Stories: The night the bed fell.   The unicorn in the garden.
The little girl and the wolf.   Memorial to a dog.   Casuals
of the keys.   The last flower.   File and forget.

Tip-toes.   OC
Monmouth Evergreen MES   7052 (1973)
Cast: Dorothy Dickson, Allan Kearns, Laddie Cliff, John
Kirby;   original London cast.
Credits: Music, George Gershwin;   lyrics, Ira Gershwin;
book, Guy Bolton and Fred Thompson.
Songs: These charming people.   That certain feeling.   It's
a great little world.   Looking for a boy.   When do we
dance?   Nice baby (come to papa).   Nightie-night.   Sweet
and low down.

To Broadway with love.   OC
Columbia OL 8030/OS   2630 (1964)
Credits: Features music of many Broadway composers;
Title theme and original material: music, Jerry Bock;
lyrics, Sheldon Harnick.

To live another summer.   OC
Buddah BDS   95004 (1972)
Cast: Rivka Raz, Aric Lavie, Yona Altari, Ili Gorlizki,
Hanan Goldblatt.
Credits: Music, Dov Seltzer;   book and lyrics, Hayim Hefer.
Songs: Son of man.   Come angel come.   The grove of euca-
lyptus.   Hasidic medley.   The boy with the fiddle.   Can
you hear my voice?   Mediterranee.   When my man returns.
Better days.   Ha'am haze.   To live another summer, to
pass another winter.   Don't destroy the world.   Give sha-
lom and sabbath to Jerusalem.   Sorry we won it.   I'm
alive.   Give me a star.

Top banana.   OC
Capitol T   11650 (1977)
Cast: Phil Silvers, Rose Marie, Jack Albertson, Lindy
 Doherty, Judy Lynn, Bob Scheerer.
Credits: Music and lyrics, Johnny Mercer;   book, Hy Kraft.
Songs: The man of the year this week.   You're so beautiful
 that. . . .   Top banana.   Elevator song.   Only if you're in
 love.   My home is in my shoes.   I fought every step of
 the way.   O. K. for TV.   Slogan song.   Meet Miss Blendo.
 Sans souci.   That's for sure.   A dog is a man's best
 friend.   A word a day.

Tovarich.   OC
Capitol TAO/STAO   1940 (1963);   Capitol STAO   11653 (1977)
Cast: Vivien Leigh, Jean Pierre Aumont, Alexander Scourby,
 Louise Troy, George S. Irving, Louise Kirtland.
Credits: Music, Lee Pockriss;   lyrics, Anne Croswell;   book,
 David Shaw.
Songs: I go to bed.   The only one.   Nitchevo.   Stuck with
 each other.   Say you'll stay.   You love me.   A small
 cartel.   Wilkes-Barre, Pa.   No! No! No!   That face.
 Uh-oh!   I know the feeling.   It used to be.   All for you.
 Make a friend.

A Tree grows in Brooklyn.   OC
Columbia ML   4405 (1950);   CSP AML   4405 (1973)
Cast: Shirley Booth, Johnny Johnston.
Credits: Music, Arthur Schwartz;   lyrics, Dorothy Fields;
 book, Betty Smith and George Abbott.
Songs: Payday.   Mine 'til Monday.   Make the man love me.
 I'm like a new broom.   Look who's dancing.   Love is the
 reason.   If you haven't got a sweetheart.   I'll buy you a
 star.   That's how it goes.   He had refinement.   Growing
 pains.   Is that my prince?   Halloween ballet.   Don't be afraid.

Turnabout.
Pelican LP   142 (1975)
Cast: Dorothy Neumann, Elsa Lanchester, Frances Osborne,
 Forman Brown.
Credits: Music and lyrics, Forman Brown.
Songs: Turnabout!   Mrs. Pettibone's chandelier.   If you
 can't get in the corners.   Claribel the Great.   Incident
 in Arch Street.   Mein Herz.   Brunhilde rides again.
 March of rhyme.   Catalogue woman.   Victory garden.
 The Doge's dilemma.   The last show.   When a lady has a piazza.

Tuscaloosa's calling me . . . but I'm not going.   OC
Vanguard VSD   79376 (1976)

Cast: Len Gochman, Patti Perkins, Renny Temple.
Credits: Music, Hank Beebe; lyrics, Bill Heyer.
Songs: Only right here in New York City. The out of town-
er. Everything you hate is right here. Delicatessen.
Tuscaloosa's calling me ... but I'm not going. Things were
out. Fugue for a menage à trois. Singles bar. Astrol-
ogy. New York from the air. Tuscaloosa tag.

Two by two. OC
Columbia S   30338 (1970)
Cast: Danny Kaye.
Credits: Music, Richard Rodgers; lyrics, Martin Charnin;
book, Peter Stone; based on The flowering peach, by
Clifford Odets.

Two gentlemen of Verona. OC
ABC/Dunhill BCSY   1001 (1971)
Cast: Clifton Davis, Raul Julia.
Credits: Music, Galt MacDermott; lyrics, John Guare;
based on Two gentlemen of Verona, by William Shakespeare.

Two gentlemen of Verona.
Kilmarnock KIL   72004 (1973)
Cast: Sheila Gibbs, Ken Lowry.
Credits: Music, Galt MacDermott; lyrics, John Guare;
based on Two gentlemen of Verona, by William Shakespeare.
Songs: Summer, summer. Love's revenge. I love my
father. Eglamour. I am not interested in love. Love
has driven me sane. Night letter. Mansion. Love me.
Who is Silvia? What does a lover pack? What a nice idea.

Two's company. OC
RCA Red Seal CBM   1-2757 (1978)
Cast: Bette Davis, Hiram Sherman, Ellen Hanley.
Credits: Music, Vernon Duke; lyrics, Ogden Nash and
Sammy Cahn; book, Charles Sherman.
Songs: Theatre is a lady. Turn me loose on Broadway.
It just occurred to me. A man's home. Roundabout.
Roll along, Sadie. Out of the clear blue sky. Esther.
Haunted hot spot. Purple rose. Just like a man.

The United States of America.
Capitol W   1573 (1961)
Cast: Stan Freberg.
Credits: Music and lyrics, Stan Freberg.

The Unsinkable Molly Brown. OC
Capitol WAO/SWAO 1509 (1960); Capitol SW 2152 (1964)
Cast: Tammy Grimes, Harve Presnell.
Credits: Music and lyrics, Meredith Willson; book, Richard
Morris.
Songs: I ain't down yet. Belly up to the bar, boys. I've
a'ready started in. I'll never say no. My own brass bed.
The Denver police. Bea-u-ti-ful people of Denver. Are
you sure? Happy birthday, Mrs. J. J. Brown. Bon jour.
If I knew. Chick-a-pen. Keep-a-hoppin! Dolce far
niente. I may never fall in love with you.

The Vagabond king.
RCA Victor LM/LSC 2509 (1961)
Cast: Mario Lanza, Judith Raskin.
Credits: Music, Rudolph Friml; book and lyrics, Brian
Hooker; based on If I were king, by Justin Huntly Mc-
Carthy.
Songs: Drinking song. Someday. Love me tonight. Only
a rose. Tomorrow. Love for sale. Hunting. Nocturne.
Huguette waltz. Song of the vagabonds.

The Vagabond king.
Monmouth Evergreen MES 7050 (1972)
Cast: Dennis King, Winnie Melville, Derek Oldham.
Credits: Music, Rudolph Friml; book and lyrics, Brian
Hooker; based on If I were king, by Justin Huntly Mc-
Carthy.
Songs: Love me tonight. Song of the vagabonds. Only a
rose.

The Vagabond king.
Decca DL 8362 (1956)
Cast: Alfred Drake.
Credits: Music, Rudolph Friml; book and lyrics, Brian
Hooker; based on If I were king, by Justin Huntly Mc-
Carthy.

Wait a minim! OC
London AMS 88002 (1966)
Cast: Andrew Tracey, Paul Tracey, Nigel Pegram, Michel
Martel, Dana Valery.

Songs: Amasalela. Ndinosara nani? Jikele maweni. Black-
white calypso. I know where I'm going. I gave my love
a cherry. Chuzi mama gwabi gwabi. Foyo. London
talking blues. Ayama. The gumboot dance. Hammer
song. Table Bay. A piece of ground. Dirty old town.
Sir Oswald Sodde. Johnny soldier. Skalo-zwi.

Walking happy. OC
Capitol VAS/SVAS 2631 (1966)
Cast: Norman Wisdom, Louise Troy, George Rose.
Credits: Music, James Van Heusen; lyrics, Sammy Cahn;
book, Roger O. Hirson and Ketti Frings; based on Hob-
son's choice, by Harold Brighouse.
Songs: Think of something else. Where was I? How d'ya
talk to a girl? If I be your best chance. What makes
it happen? Use your noggin. You're right, you're right.
I'll make a man of the man. Walking happy. I don't
think I'm in love. Such a sociable sort. It might as
well be her. People who are nice.

West Side story. OC
Columbia OL 5230 (1957); Columbia OS 2001 (1959); Co-
lumbia S 32603 (1973)
Cast: Carol Lawrence, Larry Kert, Chita Rivera, Art Smith.
Credits: Music, Leonard Bernstein; lyrics, Stephen Sond-
heim; book, Arthur Laurents.
Songs: Jet song. Something's coming. Maria. Tonight.
America. Cool. One hand, one heart. The dance at
the gymn. I feel pretty. Gee, Officer Krupke! A boy
like that. I have a love.

What it was, was love.
RCA Victor LSP 4115 (1969)
Cast: Steve Lawrence, Eydie Gorme.
Credits: Music, Gordon Jenkins.

What makes Sammy run?
Columbia KOL 6040/KOS 2040 (1964)
Cast: Steve Lawrence, Sally Ann Howes, Robert Alda,
Bernice Massi.
Credits: Music and lyrics, Ervin Drake; book, Budd and
Stuart Schulberg.

When you're in love the whole world is Jewish.
Kapp KRS 5506 (1966)

Where's Charley? OC
Monmouth Evergreen MES 7029 (1972)

Cast: Norman Wisdom; original London cast.
Credits: Music and lyrics, Frank Loesser; book George
  Abbott; based on Charley's aunt, by Brandon Thomas.
Songs: Once in love with Amy. My darling, my darling.
  Make a miracle. Lucia. Where's Charley? Better get
  out of here. The New Ashmolean Marching Society and
  Students Conservatory Band.

White Horse Inn.
Angel 35815 (1960)
Cast: Mary Thomas, Andy Cole.
Credits: Music, Ralph Benatzky and Robert Stolz; English
  book and lyrics, Harry Graham.

Whoop-up. OC
MGM E 3745 (1959)
Credits: Music, Morris Charlap.

Wild is love.
Capitol ST 408 (1970)
Cast: Patti Drew.
Credits: Music, Ray Rasch; lyrics, Dotti Wayne.

Wildcat. OC
RCA Victor LOC/LSO 1060 (1961)
Cast: Lucille Ball.
Credits: Music, Cy Coleman.

Wildflower. OC
Monmouth Evergreen MES 7052 (1973)
Cast: Kitty Reidy, Howett Worster; original London cast.
Credits: Music, Vincent Youmans and Herbert Stothart;
  book and lyrics, Otto Harbach and Oscar Hammerstein II.
Songs: Casimo. I love you. You can never blame a girl
  for dreaming. Goodbye, little rosebud. Wildflower. I
  can always find another partner. Bambalina. April blossoms.

Wish you were here. OC
RCA Victor LOC 1007 (1952); Camden 621 (1961); RCA
  Victor LSO 1108 (1965)
Cast: Sheila Bond, Jack Cassidy.
Credits: Music and lyrics, Harold Rome.

The Wiz.
Atlantic SD 18137 (1975)
Cast: Stephanie Mills, Tiger Haynes, Ted Ross, Hinton Battle.
Credits: Music/lyrics, Charlie Smalls; book, William Brown.

Songs: The feeling we once had.   Tornado.   He's the wizard.   Soon as I get home.   I was born on the day before
yesterday.   Ease on down the road.   Slide some oil to me.
I'm a mean ole lion.   Be a lion.   So you wanted to see
the wizard.   What would I do if I could feel.   Don't nobody bring me no bad news.   Everybody rejoice.   Y'all
got it.   If you believe.   Home.

The Wonderful O.   OC
Colpix CP   6000 (1963)
Cast: Burgess Meredith.
Credits: Music, J. Raymond Henderson;   book and lyrics,
J. Raymond Henderson and Burgess Meredith;   based on
The wonderful O, by James Thurber.

Wonderful town.   OC
Decca 9010 (1953); Decca 79010 (1964);   MCA Records MCA
2050 (1973)
Cast: Rosalind Russell, George Gaynes, Edith Adams.
Credits: Music, Leonard Bernstein;   lyrics, Betty Comden
and Adolph Green;   book, Joseph Fields and Jerome
Chodorov;   based on My sister Eileen, by Joseph Fields
and Jerome Chodorov.
Songs: Christopher Street.   Ohio.   One hundred easy ways.
What a waste.   A little bit in love.   Pass the football.
Conversation piece.   A quiet girl.   Conga!   My darlin'
Eileen.   Swing.   It's love.   Wrong note rag.

Wonderful town.
Columbia OL   5360 (1958);   Columbia OS   2008 (1959)
Cast: Rosalind Russell.
Credits: Music, Leonard Bernstein;   lyrics, Betty Comden
and Adolph Green;   book, Joseph Fields and Jerome
Chodorov;   based on My sister Eileen, by Joseph Fields
and Jerome Chodorov.

Words and Music.
RCA Red Seal LRL   1 5079 (1975)
Cast: Sammy Cahn, Lorna Dallas, Terry Mitchell, Laurel
Ford.
Credits: Lyrics, Sammy Cahn.
Songs: Call me irresponsible.   Shake your head.   Rhythm
is our business.   Please be kind.   I've heard that song
before.   Five minutes more.   It's been a long, long time.
It's magic.   The Christmas waltz.   Teach me tonight.
Three coins in the fountain.   Be my love.   Thoroughly
modern Millie.   All the way.   The tender trap.   Swing

low, sweet chariot. Please be kind. It's impossible. Everybody has the right to be wrong. Pap, won't you dance with me? There goes that song again. I'll never stop loving you. Day by day. The things we did last summer. Let it snow, let it snow, let it snow. Because you're mine. A touch of class. I fall in love too easily. Saturday night. I should care. Love and marriage. Until the real thing comes along. Bei mir bist du schön. I'll walk alone. Put 'em in a box. The second time around. Time after time. Come fly with me. High hopes. My kind of town.

Working. OC
Columbia PS 35411 (1978)
Credits: Music, Craig Carnelia, Micki Grant, Mary Rodgers, Susan Birkenhead, Stephen Schwartz, and James Taylor; book and lyrics, Studs Terkel; based on Terkel's book Working.
Songs: All the livelong day. Lovin' Al. The mason. Neat to be a newsboy. Nobody tells me how. Un mejor dia vendra. Just a housewife. Millwork. If I could've been. Joe. It's an art. Brother trucker. Father and sons. Cleanin' women. Something to point to.

The Yiddish are coming!
Verve V 15056 (1967)
Cast: Lou Jacobi.
Credits: Music and lyrics, Bob Booker and George Foster.

You're a good man, Charlie Brown. OC
MGM 1E-9 OC (1967)
Cast: Bill Hinnant.
Credits: Music, lyrics, and book, Clark Gesner; based on Peanuts, by Charles M. Schulz; book, John Gordon.
Songs: You're a good man, Charlie Brown. Schroeder. Snoopy. My blanket & me. Kite. Dr. Lucy. Book report. The Red Baron. T-E-A-M. Queen Lucy. Peanuts potpourri. Little known facts. Suppertime. Happiness.

Your arms too short to box with God. OC
ABC Records AB 1004 (1977)
Cast: Salome Bey, Clinton Derricks-Carroll, Delores Hall, William Hardy, Jr.

Credits: Music and lyrics, Alex Bradford and Micki Grant;
   book, Vinnette Carroll;   based on the Book of Matthew.
Songs: Beatitudes.   Good time.   Sermon.   Jesus the strang-
   er.   We are the priests and elders.   Something is wrong
   in Jerusalem.   Be careful whom you kiss.   The trial.
   It's too late Judas.   Your arms too short to box with God.
   See how they done my Lord.   Come on down.   Can't no
   grave hold my body down.   Didn't I tell you.   As long as
   I live.   Everybody has his own way.   I love you so much
   Jesus.   We're gonna have a good time.

Your own thing.   OC
RCA Victor LOC/LSO   1148 (1968)
Cast: Leland Palmer, Rusty Thacker.
Credits: Music and lyrics, Hal Hester and Danny Apolinar;
   based on Twelfth night, by William Shakespeare.

Zorba.   OC
Capitol SO   118 (1969)
Cast: Herschel Bernardi, Maria Karnilova.
Credits: Music, John Kander;   lyrics, Fred Ebb;   book,
   Joseph Stein;   adapted from Zorba the Greek, by Nikos
   Kazantzakis.
Songs: Life is.   The first time.   The top of the hill.   No
   boom boom.   The butterfly.   Goodbye, Canavaro.   Only
   love.   The bend in the road.   Y'assou.   Why can't I
   speak?   The crow.   Happy birthday to me.   I am free.

The Zulu and the zayda.   OC
Columbia KOL 6480/KOS   2880 (1965)
Cast: Menasha Skulnik.
Credits: Music and lyrics, Harold Rome.

★ COMPOSER INDEX

★ BOOK AND LYRICS WRITER INDEX

Abbott, George
  Anya
  The Boys from Syracuse
  Damn Yankees
  Fiorello
  Flora, the red menace
  On your toes
  The Pajama game
  A Tree grows in
    Brooklyn
  Where's Charley?
Abel, George
  Show biz
Adams, Lee
  All American
  Applause
  Bye bye Birdie
  Golden boy
  It's a bird, it's a plane,
    it's Superman
Adler, Richard
  Damn Yankees
  Kwamina
  The Pajama game
Anderson, Maxwell
  Lost in the stars

Apolinar, Danny
  Your own thing
Appell, Don
  Milk and honey
Arlen, Harold
  House of flowers
Aurthur, Robert Alan
  Kwamina
Barer, Marshall
  The Mad show
  Once upon a mattress
Bart, Lionel
  Oliver!
Bass, Jules
  Cricket on the hearth
Basse, Eli
  Gypsy Rose Lee re-
    members burlesque
Behrman, S. N.
  Fanny
Benson, Sally
  Seventeen
Benton, Robert
  It's a bird, it's a plane,
    it's Superman
Berlin, Irving

Gordon, John
  You're a good man,
    Charlie Brown
Graham, Harry
  Maid of the mountains
  White Horse Inn
Graham, Ronny
  Bravo Giovanni
Grant, Micki
  Don't bother me, I
    can't cope
  Your arms too short
    to box with God
Gray, Timothy
  High spirits
Green, Adolph
  Applause
  Bells are ringing
  Do-re-mi
  Fade out, fade in
  Hallelujah, baby
  Lorelei
  On the town
  On the Twentieth
    Century
  A Party
  Say, darling
  Subways are for
    sleeping
  Wonderful town
Green, Benny
  Cole
Grey, Clifford
  Sally
  The Three musketeers
Grossmith, George
  Primrose
Grudeff, Marian
  Baker Street
Guare, John
  Two gentlemen of
    Verona
Hackady, Hal
  Goodtime Charley
Haimsohn, George
  Dames at sea
Hammerstein, Oscar II

Allegro
Carmen Jones
Carousel
Cinderella
The Desert song
Flower drum song
The King and I
Me and Juliet
The New moon
Oklahoma
Pipe dream
Rose Marie
Show boat
The Sound of music
South Pacific
Sunny
Wildflower
Harbach, Otto
  The Desert song
  No, no, Nanette
  Roberta
  Rose Marie
  Sunny
  Wildflower
Harburg, E. Y.
  Bloomer girl
  Darling of the day
  Finian's rainbow
  Flahooley
  The Happiest girl in
    the world
  Jamaica
Harnick, Sheldon
  The Apple tree
  Fiddler on the roof
  Fiorello
  Rex
  The Rothschilds
  She loves me
  Tenderloin
  To Broadway with love
Harron, Donald
  Anne of Green Gables
Hart, Lorenz
  Babes in arms
  The Boys from
    Syracuse

By Jupiter
Evergreen
I married an angel
On your toes
Pal Joey
Hart, Moss
  Lady in the dark
Hart, Stan
  The Mad show
Hecht, Ben
  Hazel Flagg
Hellman, Lillian
  Candide
Henderson, J. Raymond
  The Wonderful O
Heneker, David
  Half a sixpence
  Irma la douce
Herman, Jerry
  Dear world
  Hello, Dolly
  Mack & Mabel
  Mame
  Milk and honey
  Parade
Herzig, Sid
  Bloomer girl
Hester, Hal
  Your own thing
Heyer, Bill
  Tuscaloosa's calling
    me ... but I am
    not going
Heyward, Du Bose
  Porgy and Bess
Hilliard, Bob
  Hazel, Flagg
Hirson, Roger O.
  Walking happy
Holm, John Cecil
  Best foot forward
Holt, Will
  The Me nobody knows
Hooker, Brian
  The Vagabond king
Horwitt, Arnold B.
  Plain and fancy
Hughes, Langston

Simply heaven
Street scene
Hugo & Luigi
  Maggie Flynn
Jacob, Bill
  Jimmy
Jacob, Patti
  Jimmy
Jacobs, Jim
  Grease
Jenkins, Gordon
  Our love letter
Jessel, Raymond
  Baker Street
Jones, Tom
  Celebration
  The Fantasticks
  I do! I do!
  110 in the shade
Kanin, Fay
  The Gay life
Kanin, Garson
  Do-re-mi
Kanin, Michael
  The Gay life
Kaufman, George S.
  The Bandwagon
  Of thee I sing
  Silk stockings
Kerr, Jean
  Goldilocks
Kerr, Walter
  Goldilocks
Kinoy, Ernest
  Bajour
Kirkwood, James
  A Chorus line
Kleban, Edward
  A Chorus line
Kraft, Hy
  Top banana
Kurnitz, Harry
  The Girl who came
    to supper
Lakier, Gail
  Ipi-Tombi
Lampert, Diane
  Big man

Starting here, starting
now
Manchester, Joe
The Secret life of
Walter Mitty
Mandel, Frank
The Desert song
The New moon
No, no, Nanette
Marion, George
Arabian nights
Marks, Walter
Bajour
Martin, Hugh
High spirits
Masteroff, Joe
Cabaret
She loves me
Mayer, Paul Avila
Big man
Meehan, Thomas
Annie
Mercer, Johnny
L'il Abner
St. Louis woman
Saratoga
Top banana
Meredith, Burgess
The Wonderful O
Merriam, E.
Inner city
Merrill, Robert
Carnival
Funny girl
New girl in town
Sugar
Take me along
Michaels, Sidney
Ben Franklin in Paris
Goodtime Charley
Miller, F. E.
Shuffle along
Miller, Robin
Dames at sea
Mitchell, Loften
Bubbling brown sugar
Montgomery, James

Irene
More, Julian
Irma la douce
Morgan, Al
Oh captain
Morris, Richard
The Unsinkable Molly
Brown
Myers, Henry
The Happiest girl in
the world
Nash, N. Richard
The Happy time
Nash, Ogden
The Littlest revue
Two's company
Nemiroff, Robert
Raisin
Newley, Anthony
The Roar of the
greasepaint
Stop the world, I
want to get off
Newman, David
It's a bird, it's a
plane, it's Super-
man
Nichols, Peter
Privates on parade
Norman, Monty
Irma la douce
Odets, Clifford
Golden boy
Oesterman, Phil
Let my people come
Panama, Norman
L'il Abner
Parent, Gail
Lorelei
Parker, Dorothy
Candide
Pascal, Fran
George M!
Pascal, John
George M!
Paxton, Glenn
First impressions

Porter, Cole
  Anything goes
  Can-can
  Cole
  The Decline and fall of
    the entire world as
    seen through the eyes
    of Cole Porter
  Jubilee
  Kiss me, Kate
  Nymph errant
  Out of this world
  Silk stockings
Rado, James
  DisinHAIRited
  Hair
Ragni, Gerome
  DisinHAIRitcd
  Dude
  Hair
Randall, Bob
  The Magic show
Reynolds, Dorothy
  Salad days
Rice, Elmer
  Street scene
Rice, Tim
  Jesus Christ superstar
Robin, Leo
  Gentlemen prefer
    blondes
  The Girl in pink tights
Rodgers, Richard
  Babes in arms
  By Jupiter
  I married an angel
  No strings
  On your toes
Rome, Harold
  Destry rides again
  Fanny
  I can get it for you
    wholesale
  Pins and needles
  Wish you were here
  The Zulu and the zayda
Root, Lynn
  Cabin in the sky

Rose, Patrick
  Jubalay
Ross, Jerry
  Damn Yankees
  The Pajama game
Russell, Robert
  Flora, the red menace
Ryskind, Morrie
  Of thee I sing
Saidy, Fred
  Bloomer girl
  Finian's rainbow
  Flahooley
  The Happiest girl in
    the world
  Jamaica
Samuels, Lesser
  Greenwillow
Samuelson, Laura Byers
  Shades
Schulberg, Budd
  What makes Sammy
    run?
Schulberg, Stuart
  What makes Sammy
    run?
Schuman, Earl
  The Secret life of
    Walter Mitty
Schwab, Laurence
  The New Moon
Schwartz, Arthur
  The Gay life
Schwartz, Stephen
  Godspell
  The Magic show
  Pippin
Shavelson, Melville
  Jimmy
Shaw, David
  Redhead
  Tovarich
Sheldon, Sidney
  Redhead
Sherman, Charles
  Two's company
Sherman, Richard M.
  Over here

★ PERFORMER INDEX

Ackerman, Loni
  Starting here, starting
    now
Ackland, Joss
  A Little night music
Adair, Yvonne
  Gentlemen prefer
    blondes
Adams, Edith
  Cinderella
  L'il Abner
  Les Poupées de Paris
  Wonderful town
Adrian, Max
  Candide
Albani, Emma
  Show boat
Alberghetti, Anna Maria
  Carnival
Albert, Eddie
  Miss Liberty
Albertson, Jack
  Top banana
Alda, Alan
  The Apple tree
Alda, Robert
  Guys and dolls

What makes Sammy run?
Allen, D. R.
  How to steal an election
Allen, Elizabeth
  Do I hear a waltz?
Allen, Jonelle
  Hair
Altman, Ruth
  The Boy friend
Alvarez, Carmen
  The Decline and fall of
    the entire world as
    seen through the eyes
    of Cole Porter
Ameche, Don
  Goldilocks
  Silk stockings
Andreas, Christine
  My fair lady
Andrews, George Lee
  Starting here, starting
    now
Andrews, Julie
  The Boy friend
  Camelot
  Cinderella
  My fair lady

A Hand is on the gate
Bikel, Theodore
  The King and I
  The Sound of music
Blaine, Vivian
  Guys and dolls
  Say, darling
Bliss, Helena
  Song of Norway
Blyden, Larry
  The Apple tree
Bolger, Ray
  All American
Bond, Sheila
  Wish you were here
Bonerz, Peter
  Story theatre
Booke, Sorrell
  Finian's rainbow
Booth, Shirley
  By the beautiful sea
  Juno
  A Tree grows in
    Brooklyn
Bosley, Tom
  Fiorello
Bostwick, Barry
  Grease
Bracken, Eddie
  archy and mehitabel
Bradford, Alex
  Black nativity
  Don't bother me, I
    can't cope
Brawner, Hilda
  The Elephant calf
Brennan, Eileen
  Little Mary Sunshine
Brennan, Maureen
  Candide
Brenner, Yul
  The King and I
Brice, Carol
  Finian's rainbow
Bronhill, June
  Bitter sweet
  The Desert song
Brooks, Lawrence

  Song of Norway
Brotherson, Eric
  Gentlemen prefer blondes
Brown, Anne
  Porgy and Bess
Brown, Forman
  Turnabout
Brown, Gloria
  Oliver!
Brown, Oscar
  Joy
Browne, Roscoe Lee
  A Hand is on the gate
Brubeck, Dave
  The Real ambassadors
Brubeck, Iola
  The Real ambassadors
Bruce, Carol
  Show boat
Brune, Adrienne
  The Three musketeers
Bryant, J. D.
  Jesus Christ superstar
Burnett, Carol
  Fade out, fade in
  Once upon a mattress
  Three billion millionaires
Burns, David
  Hello, Dolly
  The Music man
Burton, Richard
  Camelot
Caesar, Sid
  Little me
Cahn, Sammy
  Words and music
Calloway, Cab
  Blackbirds of 1928
  Hello, Dolly
Calvin, Henry
  Kismet
Camp, Hamid Hamilton
  Story theatre
Capers, Virginia
  Raisin
Cardinall, Robert
  Bitter sweet
Carey, Thomas

Deems, Mickey
  Anything goes
Demas, Carole
  Grease
  How to steal an election
Derr, Richard
  Plain and fancy
Derricks-Carroll, Clinton
  Your arms too short to
    box with God
Desmond, Johnny
  Say, darling
Dickey, Annamary
  Allegro
Dickson, Dorothy
  Sally
  Tip-toes
Diener, Joan
  Kismet
  Man of La Mancha
Dishy, Bob
  By Jupiter
  Flora, the red menace
Dixon, Lee
  Oklahoma
Doherty, Lindy
  Top banana
Donaldson, Norma
  Guys and dolls
Douglas, Melvyn
  Juno
Douglass, Stephen
  Damn Yankees
  The Golden apple
  Show boat
Drake, Alfred
  Carousel
  Gigi
  Kean
  Kismet
  Kiss me, Kate
  Oklahoma
  The Vagabond king
Drew, Eleanor
  Salad days
Drew, Patti
  Wild is love

Duncan, Sandy
  The Boy friend
Duncan, Todd
  Lost in the stars
  Porgy and Bess
Dussault, Nancy
  Bajour
Dyson, Ronald
  Hair
Eddy, Nelson
  The Desert song
  I married an angel
  Oklahoma
Ellington, Duke
  Blackbirds of 1928
Elliott, Shaun
  Jacques Brel is alive
    and well and living
    in Paris
Evans, Wilbur
  By the beautiful sea
Everhart, Rex
  1776
Ewell, Tom
  A Thurber carnival
Fabray, Nanette
  High button shoes
  Make a wish
  Mr. President
Fargé, Anne
  Les Poupées de Paris
Fenholt, Jeff
  Jesus Christ superstar
Ferrer, José
  The Girl who came to
    supper
  Oh captain
Flanders, Michael
  At the drop of a hat
  At the drop of another
    hat
Ford, Laurel
  Words and music
Ford, Paul
  A Thurber carnival
Foster, Stuart
  Oklahoma

Canterbury tales
Greenwood, Charlotte
Out of this world
Grey, Joel
Cabaret
George M!
Goodtime Charley
Griffith, Andy
Destry rides again
Grimes, Tammy
High spirits
The Unsinkable Molly
Brown
Groseclose, Frank
The Elephant calf
Guardino, Harry
Anyone can whistle
Guillaume, Robert
Big man
Guys and dolls
Hackett, Buddy
I had a ball
Hale, Binnie
No, no Nanette
Sunny
Hall, Adelaide
Blackbirds of 1928
Hall, Delores
Your arms too short to
box with God
Hall, Juanita
Flower drum song
South Pacific
Hamilton, Barbara
Anne of Green Gables
Hampshire, Keith
Oops!
Hanley, Ellen
Fiorello
Two's company
Hardy, William, Jr.
Your arms too short
to box with God
Harris, Barbara
The Apple tree
On a clear day you
can see forever

Harris, Julie
Skyscraper
Harris, Phil
Gigi
My fair lady
Paint your wagon
Harrison, Rex
My fair lady
Hartman, Paul
Of thee I sing
Haskell, David
Godspell
Haskell, Jack
Mr. President
Haworth, Jill
Cabaret
Hayes, Richard
The Nervous set
Haynes, Tiger
The Wiz
Head, Murray
Jesus Christ superstar
Hecht, Paul
The Rothschilds
1776
Heitgerd, Don
Cinderella
Henderson, Florence
The Girl who came to
supper
Oklahoma
South Pacific
Henson, Leslie
Primrose
Sally
Hepburn, Katharine
Coco
Hickey, William
The Decline and fall of
the entire world as
seen through the eyes
of Cole Porter
Hilda, Irene
Can-can
Hill, Ruby
St. Louis woman
Hinnant, Bill

The Sound of music
Katz, Mickey
  Hello, Solly!
Kaye, Danny
  Jubilee
  Three billion millionaires
  Two by two
Kearns, Allan
  Tip-toes
Keel, Howard
  Kiss me, Kate
  Saratoga
Keeler, Ruby
  No, no, Nanette
Kellogg, Lynn
  Hair
Kelly, Gene
  Les Poupées de Paris
Kelly, Patsy
  Irene
  No, no, Nanette
Kelton, Pert
  The Music man
Kennedy, Jaye
  Jesus Christ superstar
Kercheval, Ken
  Berlin to Broadway with
    Kurt Weill
Kermoyan, Michael
  Anya
Kernan, David
  A Little night music
  Side by side by Sondheim
Kert, Larry
  West Side story
Kiley, Richard
  I had a ball
  Kismet
  Man of La Mancha
  Redhead
King, Dennis
  The Three musketeers
  The Vagabond king
Kirby, John
  Tip-toes
Kirk, Lisa
  Kiss me, Kate

Mack & Mabel
Kirsten, Dorothy
  The Desert song
  Kismet
  The New moon
  The Student prince
Kirtland, Louise
  Tovarich
Kitt, Eartha
  New faces of 1952
Klugman, Jack
  Gypsy
Kneebone, Tom
  The Apple tree
Kruschen, Jack
  I can get it for you
    wholesale
Laine, Cleo
  Show boat
Lanchester, Elsa
  Elsa Lanchester herself
  Turnabout
Lander, Judy
  Berlin to Broadway with
    Kurt Weill
Lang, Harold
  The Decline and fall of
    the entire world as
    seen through the eyes
    of Cole Porter
  I can get it for you
    wholesale
  Make a wish
  Pal Joey
Lanning, Jerry
  Berlin to Broadway
    with Kurt Weill
Lansbury, Angela
  Anyone can whistle
  Dear world
  Gypsy
  Mame
Lanza, Mario
  The Desert song
  The Student prince
  The Vagabond king
Larsen, William

McGuire, Biff
  Finian's rainbow
McKeever, Jacquelyn
  Oh captain
McKellar, Kenneth
  Kismet
McKenzie, Julia
  Side by side by Sondheim
McLerie, Allyn
  Miss Liberty
McMartin, John
  Follies
  Sweet Charity
McNeil, Claudia
  Simply heaven
MacRae, Gordon
  The Desert song
  Kismet
  The New moon
  Roberta
  The Student prince
Maharis, George
  Three billion millionaires
Mako
  Pacific overtures
Mansfield, Jane
  Les Poupées de Paris
Marker, Preshy
  A Funny thing happened
    on the way to the
    Forum
Markham, Monte
  Irene
Marlowe, Marion
  The Sound of music
Martel, Michel
  Wait a minim!
Martin, Connie
  Oops!
Martin, Leila
  The Rothschilds
Martin, Mary
  Annie get your gun
  Anything goes
  Babes in arms
  The Bandwagon
  Girl crazy

Hello, Dolly
I do! I do!
Jennie
Jubilee
Pacific 1860
Peter Pan
The Sound of music
South Pacific
Martin, Millicent
  Side by side by Sondheim
Martin, Tony
  Les Poupées de Paris
Martin, Virginia
  How to succeed in
    business without
    really trying
  Little me
Marx, Groucho
  An Evening with Groucho
Mason, Marlyn
  How now, Dow Jones
Massey, Daniel
  Gigi
  She loves me
Massi, Bernice
  What makes Sammy run?
Mathews, Carmen
  Dear world
Matthews, Inez
  Lost in the stars
Matthews, Jessie
  Evergreen
Mayo, Mary
  Kiss me, Kate
Melchior, Lauritz
  The Student prince
Melton, James
  Show boat
Melville, Winnie
  The Vagabond king
Meredith, Burgess
  The Wonderful O
Merman, Ethel
  Annie get your gun
  Call me madam
  Gypsy
  Jubilee

Poole, Roy
  1776
Porter, Cole
  Jubilee
Powell, Jane
  Gigi
  My fair lady
  Paint your wagon
Prémice, Josephine
  Bubbling brown sugar
  A Hand is on the gate
Presnell, Harve
  The Unsinkable Molly
    Brown
Preston, Robert
  Ben Franklin in Paris
  I do! I do!
  Mack & Mabel
  The Music man
Price, Gilbert
  Promenade
Price, Vincent
  Darling of the day
Prior, Allan
  The Student prince
Prochnik, Bruce
  Oliver!
Quayle, Anna
  Stop the world, I want
    to get off
Rado, James
  DisinHAIRited
  Hair
Ragni, Gerome
  DisinHAIRited
  Hair
Raitt, John
  Annie get your gun
  Carousel
  Oklahoma
  Show boat
Ramsey, Logan
  The Elephant calf
Randall, Tony
  Oh captain
Randolph James
  Guys and dolls

Raskin, Judith
  The Desert song
  The Vagabond king
Ravenscroft, Thurl
  The Desert song
Reardon, John
  Lady in the dark
  On the town
Reed, Vivian
  Bubbling brown sugar
Reidy, Kitty
  Wildflower
Reilly, Charles Nelson
  How to succeed in
    business without
    really trying
Reinking, Ann
  Goodtime Charley
Remick, Lee
  Anyone can whistle
Resnik, Regina
  Kismet
Revill, Clive
  Oliver!
Reynolds, Debbie
  Irene
Richards, Donald
  Finian's rainbow
Richardson, Ian
  My fair lady
Ritchard, Cyril
  The Happiest girl in
    the world
  Peter Pan
  The Roar of the
    greasepaint
  Sugar
Ritter, Thelma
  New girl in town
Rivera, Chita
  Bajour
  Bye bye Birdie
  Chicago
  West Side story
Roane, Frank
  Lost in the stars
Roberts, Anthony

How now, Dow Jones
Roberts, Joan
  Oklahoma
  Roberta
Roberts, Tony
  Sugar
Robeson, Paul
  Show boat
Roche, Eugene
  The Secret life of
    Walter Mitty
Rodgers, Eileen
  Anything goes
Rogers, Ginger
  Cinderella
Rome, Harold
  Fanny
Rose, George
  Canterbury tales
  My fair lady
  Walking happy
Rose Marie
  Top banana
Rose, Patrick
  Jubalay
Ross, Jamie
  Oh Coward!
Ross, Ted
  The Wiz
Roth Lillian
  I can get it for you
    wholesale
  70, girls 70
Rounseville, Robert
  Candide
  The Student prince
Routledge, Patricia
  Darling of the day
Royle, Derek
  Show boat
Rubinstein, John
  Pippin
Ruick, Barbara
  Cinderella
  Oh, Kay!
Russell, Rosalind
  Wonderful town

Ryan, Irene
  Pippin
San Juan, Olga
  Paint your wagon
Sands, Robert
  The Desert song
Saunders, Gertrude
  Shuffle along
Saxon, Luther
  Carmen Jones
Schaal, Richard
  Story theatre
Schaeffer, Sandra
  Promenade
Scheerer, Bob
  Top banana
Scott, Bonnie
  How to succeed in
    business without
    really trying
Scourby, Alexander
  Tovarich
Seal, Elizabeth
  Irma la douce
Segal, Vivienne
  Pal Joey
Seitz, Tani
  The Nervous set
Shafer, Robert
  Song of Norway
Shelton, Reid
  Annie
Sherman, Hiram
  Anne of Green Gables
  How now, Dow Jones
  Two's company
Shore, Dinah
  Call me madam
Shuman, Mort
  Jacques Brel is alive
    and well and living
    in Paris
Sicari, Joseph R.
  Dames at sea
Siepi, Cesare
  Bravo Giovanni
Silvers, Phil

Do-re-mi
High button shoes
Les Poupées de Paris
Top banana
Simmons, Jean
  A Little night music
Sissle, Noble
  Shuffle along
Sivuca
  Joy
Skulnik, Menasha
  The Zulu and the zayda
Slezak, Walter
  Fanny
Smith, Alexis
  Follies
Smith, Art
  West Side story
Smith, Loring
  The Gay life
Smith, Muriel
  Carmen Jones
Sothern, Ann
  Lady in the dark
Soules, Dale
  The Magic show
Stadlen, Lewis J.
  Candide
Stanley, Pat
  Goldilocks
Stapley, Diane
  Jubalay
Stevens, Craig
  Here's love
Stevens, Risë
  The King and I
  Lady in the dark
  Show boat
Stewart, Melvin
  Simply heaven
Stewart, Princess
  Black nativity
Stickney, Dorothy
  Cinderella
Stiers, David Ogden
  The Magic show
Stone, Elly

Jacques Brel is alive
  and well and living
  in Paris
Stoska, Polyna
  Street scene
Streisand, Barbra
  Funny girl
  I can get it for you
    wholesale
Stritch, Elaine
  Company
  Goldilocks
  Sail away
Stroud, Gregory
  Sally
Sullivan, Brian
  Street scene
Sumac, Yma
  Flahooley
Suzuki, Pat
  Flower drum song
Swados, Elizabeth
  Runaways
Swann, Donald
  At the drop of a hat
  At the drop of another
    hat
Swenson, Inga
  Baker Street
Tabbert, William
  South Pacific
Taylor, Sam, Jr.
  Jesus Christ superstar
Temple, Renny
  Tuscaloosa's calling
    me ... but I am
    not going
Thacker, Rusty
  Your own thing
Thomas, Danny
  Cricket on the hearth
Thomas, Hugh
  The Fantasticks
Thomas, Mary
  White Horse Inn
Thomas, Terry
  Three billion millionaires

★ SONG INDEX

All is well in the sky
   Promenade
All of you
   Silk stockings
All our friends
   George M!
All that jazz
   Chicago
All the dearly beloved
   I do! I do!
All the time
   Oh captain
All through the night
   Anything goes
Alleluia
   Candide
Almost like being in love
   Brigadoon
Alone
   Jacques Brel is alive
      and well and living
      in Paris
Alone too long
   By the beautiful sea
Always mademoiselle
   Coco
Always true to you
   Kiss me, Kate
America
   West Side story
Among my yesterdays
   The Happy time
Amsterdam
   Jacques Brel is alive
      and well and living
      in Paris
Anatavka
   Fiddler on the roof
And I was beautiful
   Dear world
And this is my beloved
   Kismet
Another autumn
   Paint your wagon
Another day
   Hallelujah, baby
Another hundred people

Company
Another op'nin', another show
   Kiss me, Kate
Another time, another place
   Kwamina
Any little fish
   Cowardy custard
Any place I hang my hat
   is home
   St. Louis woman
Anyone would love you
   Destry rides again
Anything goes
   Cole
Anything you can do
   Annie get your gun
April blossoms
   Wildflower
April song
   Canterbury tales
Aquarius
   Hair
Are we downhearted
   Oh, what a lovely war
Are you sure?
   The Unsinkable Molly
      Brown
As long as he needs me
   Oliver!
As long as there's a mother
   First impressions
As on through the seasons
   we sail
   Silk stockings
As once I loved you
   Rex
At the fair
   Show boat
At the field of cloth of gold
   Rex
Auditions
   Cowardy custard
Auto da fe
   Candide
Away from you
   Rex
Baby!

Blackbirds of 1928
Baby dream your dream
  Sweet Charity
Baby June and her newsboys
  Gypsy
Baby, talk to me
  Bye bye Birdie
Bachelor's dance
  Jacques Brel is alive
   and well and living
   in Paris
Backstage babble
  Applause
Bad companions
  Goldilocks
Bali, Ha'i
  South Pacific
Ballad of the garment trade
  I can get it for you
   wholesale
Bamboo cage
  House of flowers
Bandana days
  Shuffle along
The Banshee sisters
  A Party
Barbary coast
  Girl crazy
The barber's song
  Man of La Mancha
Barcelona
  Company
Bargaining
  Do I hear a waltz?
The Baroness Bazooka
  A Party
Baubles, bangles and beads
  Kismet
Bazaar of the caravans
  Kismet
Be a clown
  Cole
Be a Santa
  Subways are for sleeping
Be back soon
  Oliver!
Be kind to your parents

Fanny
Be like the bluebird
  Anything goes
Be my love
  Words and music
The beast in you
  Goldilocks
Beat dat rhythm on a drum
  Carmen Jones
Beatnik love affair
  Cowardy custard
Beautiful, beautiful world
  The Apple tree
The beautiful land
  The Roar of the grease-
   paint
Bea-u-ti-ful people of Denver
  The Unsinkable Molly
   Brown
Beautiful through and through
  Sugar
The beauty that drives men
  mad
  Sugar
Because you're mine
  Words and music
Been a long day
  How to succeed in
   business without
   really trying
Before I gaze at you again
  Camelot
Before the parade passes by
  Hello, Dolly
The begat
  Finian's rainbow
Begin the beguine
  Cole
The beguine
  Dames at sea
Being alive
  Company
Being good
  Hallelujah, baby
Belly up to the bar, boys
  The Unsinkable Molly
   Brown

Beloved
    The Student prince
The bend in the road
    Zorba
The best night of my life
    Applause
The best thing for you
    Call me madam
The best of all possible
    worlds
    Candide
The best years of his life
    Lady in the dark
Better get out of here
    Where's Charley?
Bewitched
    Pal Joey
Bianca
    Kiss me, Kate
Bidin' my time
    Girl crazy
Big "D"
    The Most happy fella
Big spender
    Sweet Charity
Big time
    Mack & Mabel
Bill
    Show boat
Billie
    George M!
Birthday song
    Fanny
Black boys
    Hair
Bloody Mary
    South Pacific
The bloom is off the rose
    The Gay life
Blow Gabriel blow
    Anything goes
Blow high, blow low
    Carousel
Bon jour
    The Unsinkable Molly
        Brown
Bon voyage

Anything goes
    Candide
Bosom buddies
    Mame
Boy for sale
    Oliver!
A boy like that
    West Side story
A boy like you
    Street scene
Boy wanted
    Primrose
Boy! What love has done
    to me
    Girl crazy
Bride and groom
    Oh, Kay!
Bring me my bride
    A Funny thing happened
        on the way to the
        Forum
Bring on the girls
    Side by side by Sondheim
Broadway baby
    Dames at sea
    Follies
Bronco busters
    Girl crazy
Bronxville Darby and Joan
    Cowardy custard
Brotherhood of man
    How to succeed in
        business without
        really trying
Brush up your Shakespeare
    Kiss me, Kate
Brussels
    Jacques Brel is alive
        and well and living
        in Paris
Buckle down Winsocki
    Best foot forward
The bulls
    Jacques Brel is alive
        and well and living
        in Paris
The bum won

Brigadoon
Drink, drink, drink
The Student prince
Drop that name
Bells are ringing
The dubbing
Man of La Mancha
Dulcinea
Man of La Mancha
Each tomorrow morning
Dear world
Eastern and western love
The desert song
The eagle and me
Bloomer girl
The earth and other minor
things
Gigi
Easy to be hard
Hair
Eat a little something
I can get it for you
wholesale
The echo waltz
Dames at sea
Edelweiss
The Sound of music
Electric blues
Hair
Elegance
Hello, Dolly
Elizabeth
Rex
Embraceable you
Girl crazy
Empty bed blues
Me and Bessie
Empty pockets filled with
love
Mr. President
An English teacher
Bye bye Birdie
Entrance of Eric
Jubilee
Esther
Two's company
Evelina

Bloomer girl
Every day a little death
A Little night music
Every little while
The Three musketeers
Every street's a boulevard
in old New York
Hazel Flagg
Everybody likes you
Carnival
Everybody ought to have
a maid
A Funny thing happened
on the way to the
Forum
Everybody says don't
Anyone can whistle
Everybody's got a home
but me
Pipe dream
Everything's alright
Jesus Christ superstar
Everything's coming up
roses
Gypsy
Everything's great
Golden boy
Ev'ry time
Best foot forward
Ev'rybod-ee who's anybod-ee
Jubilee
Exanaplanetooch
Hair
Experiment
Nymph errant
Exploitation record
Blackbirds of 1928
Extraordinary
Pippin
A fact can be a beautiful
thing
Promises, promises
Fair warning
Destry rides again
Faith
I had a ball
Falling in love with love

The French lesson
  A Party
French military marching
    song
  The Desert song
Friendship
  Anything goes
From afar
  Rex
From now till forever
  Cyrano
From the first time
  The Gay life
From this day on
  Brigadoon
From this moment on
  Cole
Fugue for tinhorns
  Guys and dolls
Funeral tango
  Jacques Brel is alive
    and well and living
    in Paris
Funky world
  Joy
Funny honey
  Chicago
A funny thing happened
  I can get it for you
    wholesale
Gabrielle
  Coco
The game
  Damn Yankees
A game of poker
  Saratoga
Garbage
  Dear world
Gary, Indiana
  The Music man
Gaudeamus igitur
  The Student prince
Gee, Officer Krupke!
  West Side story
The gentleman is a dope
  Allegro
Gentleman Jimmy
  Fiorello

A gentleman never falls
  wildly in love
  First impressions
Gesticulate
  Kismet
Get me to the church on
    time
  My fair lady
Gethsemane
  Jesus Christ superstar
Getting married today
  Company
Getting to know you
  The King and I
A gift today
  I can get it for you
    wholesale
Gimme some
  Golden boy
Girl of the moment
  Lady in the dark
The girl on the prow
  The New moon
The girl that I marry
  Annie get your gun
Girls like me
  Subways are for sleeping
Give England strength
  The Rothschilds
Give him the oo-la-la
  The Decline and fall of
    the entire world as
    seen through the eyes
    of Cole Porter
Give it all you got
  Oh captain
Give me a star
  To live another summer
Give my regards to Broadway
  George M!
Give the little lady
  Goldilocks
The glamorous life
  A Little night music
Gliding through my memoree
  Flower drum song
Glitter and be gay
  Candide

The Boys from Syracuse
He loves and she loves
  Funny face
Heart
  Damn Yankees
The heart has won the game
  First impressions
Heart of stone
  Goldilocks
The heather on the hill
  Brigadoon
Heaven hop
  Anything goes
Heaven on earth
  Oh, Kay!
Heaven on their minds
  Jesus Christ superstar
Hello, hello there!
  Bells are ringing
Hello, I love you, goodbye
  The Secret life of
    Walter Mitty
Hello, young lovers
  The King and I
Henry Street
  Funny girl
Her face
  Carnival
Here and now
  The Girl who came to
    supper
Here comes the sun
  Story theatre
Here in Eden
  The Apple tree
Here we are again
  Do I hear a waltz?
Here's to your illusions
  Flahooley
Hernando's hideaway
  The Pajama game
He's back
  The Happy time
He's good for me
  Seesaw
He's in love
  Kismet

He's only wonderful
  Flahooley
Hey, madame
  Oh captain
Hey there
  Pajama game
Hey, why not!
  Sugar
High and low
  The Bandwagon
High hopes
  Words and music
The highest judge of all
  Carousel
His eye is on the sparrow
  Bubbling brown sugar
His love makes me beautiful
  Funny girl
Home
  The Wiz
Home again
  Fiorello
Home sweet heaven
  High spirits
Homesick blues
  Gentlemen prefer blondes
Homework
  Miss Liberty
Honestly sincere
  Bye bye Birdie
Honey bun
  South Pacific
Honey in the honeycomb
  Cabin in the sky
The honeymoon is over
  I do! I do!
Honeysuckle Rose
  Ain't misbehavin'
  Bubbling brown sugar
Hoops
  The Bandwagon
Hosanna
  Jesus Christ superstar
The Hostess with the mostes'
  on the ball
  Call me madam
A house in town

Hallelujah, baby
I don't remember you
   The Happy time
I don't think I'm in love
   Walking happy
I don't want to know
   Dear world
I enjoy being a girl
   Flower drum song
I feel like I'm fixin' to die
   rag
   Story theatre
I feel merely marvelous
   Redhead
I feel pretty
   West Side story
I feel sorry for the girl
   First impressions
I fought every step of the
   way
   Top banana
I gave my love a cherry
   Wait a minim!
I get a kick out of you
   Anything goes
I got a song
   Bloomer girl
I got beauty
   Out of this world
I got life
   Hair
I got lost in his arms
   Annie get your gun
I got plenty o' nuttin'
   Porgy and Bess
I got rhythm
   Girl crazy
I got the sun in the morning
   Annie get your gun
I gotta keep movin'
   Don't bother me, I
      can't cope
I guess I'll miss the man
   Pippin
I had myself a true love
   St. Louis woman
I happen to like New York

Cole
I hate him
   Carnival
I hate men
   Kiss me, Kate
I have a love
   West Side story
I have dreamed
   The King and I
I have the room above her
   Show boat
I have to tell you
   Fanny
I just can't wait
   Subways are for sleeping
I know the feeling
   Tovarich
I know your kind
   Destry rides again
I like you
   Fanny
I love a cop
   Fiorello
I love Louisa
   The Bandwagon
I love my wife
   I do! I do!
I love Paris
   Can-can
I love to cry at weddings
   Sweet Charity
I love travelling
   Cowardy custard
I love what I'm doing
   Gentlemen prefer blondes
I loved
   Jacques Brel is alive and
      well and living in Paris
I loved her too
   Street scene
I loved you once in silence
   Camelot
I make hay when the moon
   shines
   Primrose
I may never fall in love
   with you

If love were all
  Bitter sweet
If mama was married
  Gypsy
If my friends could see
  me now
  Sweet Charity
If that was love
  New girl in town
If this isn't love
  Finian's rainbow
If we only have love
  Jacques Brel is alive
    and well and living
    in Paris
If you believe
  The Wiz
If you could see her
  Cabaret
If you haven't got a
  sweetheart
  A Tree grows in
    Brooklyn
If you're in love, you'll
  waltz
  Rio Rita
I'll be hard to handle
  Roberta
I'll be your baby tonight
  Story theatre
I'll buy you a star
  A Tree grows in
    Brooklyn
I'll follow my secret heart
  Conversation piece
I'll go home with Bonnie
  Jean
  Brigadoon
I'll know
  Guys and dolls
I'll never be jealous again
  The Pajama game
I'll never fall in love again
  Promises, promises
I'll never say no
  The Unsinkable Molly
    Brown

I'll remember her
  The Girl who came to
    supper
I'll see you again
  Bitter sweet
I'll tell the man in the
  street
  I married an angel
I'll walk with God
  The Student prince
I'm a bad, bad man
  Annie get your gun
I'm always chasing rainbows
  Irene
I'm an Indian too
  Annie get your gun
I'm an ordinary man
  My fair lady
I'm a'tingle, I'm a'glow
  Gentlemen prefer blondes
I'm blue
  On the town
I'm calm
  A Funny thing happened
    on the way to the
    Forum
I'm fascinating
  All American
I'm glad I'm not young
  anymore
  Gigi
I'm goin' back
  Bells are ringing
I'm gonna leave off wearing
  my shoes
  House of flowers
I'm gonna sit right down
  and write myself a letter
  Ain't misbehavin'
I'm gonna wash that man
  right outa my hair
  South Pacific
I'm in love! I'm in love!
  The Rothschilds
I'm just taking my time
  Subways are for sleeping
I'm just wild about Harry

It's alright with me
    Can-can
It's always love
    Sugar
It's bad for me
    Nymph errant
It's delightful down in Chile
    Gentlemen prefer blondes
It's de-lovely
    Anything goes
It's fun to think
    All American
It's good to be alive
    New girl in town
It's high time
    Gentlemen prefer blondes
It's love
    Wonderful town
It's never quite the same
    Oh captain
It's never too late to fall
    in love
    The Boy friend
It's not where you start
    Seesaw
It's she and it's me
    Cyrano
It's so simple
    Baker Street
It's today
    Mame
It's you
    Dames at sea
    The Music man
I've a'ready started in
    The Unsinkable Molly
    Brown
I've been invited to a party
    The Girl who came to
    supper
I've been there and I'm back
    Oh captain
I've come to wive it wealthily
    in Padua
    Kiss me, Kate
I've confessed to the breeze
    No, No, Nanette

I've got to find a man
    Carnival
I've got what you want
    The Apple tree
I've got you to lean on
    Anyone can whistle
I've grown accustomed
    to her face
    My fair lady
I've just seen her
    All American
I've never been in love
    before
    Guys and dolls
I've never said I love you
    Dear world
Jackie
    Jacques Brel is alive
    and well and living
    in Paris
Jeannie's packin' up
    Brigadoon
Jet song
    West Side story
Joey, Joey, Joey
    The Most happy fella
John nineteen: forty-one
    Jesus Christ superstar
Johnny one note
    Babes in arms
Josephine
    Silk stockings
Jubilation T. Cornpone
    L'il Abner
Judas' death
    Jesus Christ superstar
June is bustin' out all over
    Carousel
Just a kiss apart
    Gentlemen prefer blondes
Just a little joint with a
    juke box
    Best foot forward
Just by your example
    Evergreen
Just in time
    Bells are ringing

Candide
Life is like a train
  On the Twentieth Century
The life of the party
  The Happy time
Life upon the wicked stage
  Show boat
Like a god
  Flower drum song
Li'l black sheep
  Cabin in the sky
Little bird, little bird
  Man of La Mancha
Little biscuit
  Jamaica
A little bit in love
  Wonderful town
A little bit of good
  Chicago
A little brains, a little talent
  Damn Yankees
Little fish in a big pond
  Miss Liberty
A little girl from Little Rock
  Gentlemen prefer blondes
A little gossip
  Man of La Mancha
The little gray house
  Lost in the stars
Little lamb
  Gypsy
A little more heart
  Hazel Flagg
The little things you do
  together
  Company
Little tin box
  Fiorello
Live a little
  How now, Dow Jones
Live and let live
  Can-can
Live, laugh, love
  Follies
Liza crossing the ice
  Bloomer girl
London at night

Cowardy custard
London is a little bit of
  all right
  Cowardy custard
London pride
  Cowardy custard
London talking blues
  Wait a minim!
Lonely
  The Girl who came to
  supper
The lonely goatherd
  The sound of music
Lonely house
  Street scene
Lonely town
  On the town
Long before I knew you
  Bells are ringing
Look at 'er
  New girl in town
Look for the silver lining
  Sally
Look to the rainbow
  Finian's rainbow
Look who's dancing
  A Tree grows in Brooklyn
Look who's in love
  Redhead
A lopsided bus
  Pipe dream
The Lorelei
  Sally
Lorna's here
  Golden boy
Losing my mind
  Side by side by Sondheim
Lost in loveliness
  The Girl in pink tights
The lost word
  A Party
A lot of livin' to do
  Bye bye Birdie
Louisa
  Cowardy custard
Love and marriage
  Words and music

Man for sale
  Bloomer girl
The man I used to be
  Pipe dream
The man in my life
  Saratoga
The man in the moon
  Mame
The man of the year this
    week
  Top banana
Man say
  Raisin
Manchester
  Hair
Many a new day
  Oklahoma
Many moons ago
  Once upon a mattress
Marathon
  Jacques Brel is alive
    and well and living
    in Paris
March of the musketeers
  The Three musketeers
March of the Siamese
    children
  The King and I
Mardi gras
  House of flowers
Margot
  The Desert song
Maria
  The Sound of music
  West Side story
Marian, the librarian
  The Music man
Marianne
  The New moon
Marieke
  Jacques Brel is alive
    and well and living
    in Paris
Marie's law
  Fiorello
Marriage is for old folks
  The Secret life of
    Walter Mitty

Married
  Cabaret
Marry the man today
  Guys and dolls
Marrying for love
  Call me madam
Mary
  George M!
Mary make-believe
  Cowardy custard
Matchmaker, matchmaker
  Fiddler on the roof
Mathilde
  Jacques Brel is alive
    and well and living
    in Paris
Maybe
  Oh, Kay!
Me and Marie
  Jubilee
Me and my baby
  Chicago
Me and my town
  Anyone can whistle
Mean to me
  Ain't misbehavin'
Measure the valleys
  Raisin
Meeskite
  Cabaret
Melinda
  On a clear day you can
    see forever
Melt us
  All American
Men about town
  Cowardy custard
Metaphor
  The Fantasticks
The Midas touch
  Bells are ringing
Mira
  Carnival
Miracle of miracles
  Fiddler on the roof
Miracle song
  Anyone can whistle
Miss Marmelstein

The King and I
My love
Candide
My man's gone now
Porgy and Bess
My mother's wedding day
Brigadoon
My name
Oliver!
My own best friend
Chicago
My own brass bed
The Unsinkable Molly
Brown
My own morning
Hallelujah, baby
My ship
Lady in the dark
My state
Here's love
My sword and I
The Three musketeers
My time of day
Guys and dolls
My town
George M!
My way
The Roar of the
greasepaint
My white knight
The Music man
My wish
Here's love
Namely you
L'il Abner
The name's La Guardia
Fiorello
Napoleon
Jamaica
Naughty baby
Primrose
Near to you
Damn Yankees
Necessity
Finian's rainbow
Nellie Kelly, I love you
George M!

Never, never land
Peter Pan
Never say no
The Fantasticks
Never too late for love
Fanny
Never was born
Bloomer girl
Never will I marry
Greenwillow
Nevermore
Conversation piece
The New Ashmolean
Marching Society and
Students Conservatory
Band
Where's Charley?
A new life coming
Starting here, starting
now
New sun in the sky
The Bandwagon
New York, New York
On the town
New York poverty
Cowardy custard
Next
Jacques Brel is alive
and well and living
in Paris
Night and day
Cole
Night of my nights
Kismet
Night song
Golden boy
The night they invented
champagne
Gigi
Nightlife
All American
Nina, I like America
Cowardy custard
No more
Golden boy
No one'll ever love you
Goldilocks

Once in love with Amy
  Where's Charley?
Once knew a fella
  Destry rides again
Once upon a time
  All American
Once upon a time today
  Call me madam
One
  A Chorus line
One alone
  The Desert song
One boy
  Bye bye Birdie
One flower in your garden
  The Desert song
One hallow'een
  Applause
One hand, one heart
  West Side story
One hundred easy ways
  Wonderful town
One kiss
  The New moon
  The Three musketeers
One last kiss
  Bye bye Birdie
One life to live
  Lady in the dark
One man ain't quite enough
  House of flowers
One of a kind
  Applause
One person
  Dear world
Only a rose
  The Vagabond king
The only home I know
  Shenandoah
Only if you're in love
  Top banana
Only love
  Zorba
The only one
  Tovarich
Oom-pah-pah
  Oliver!

Open a new window
  Mame
An ordinary couple
  The sound of music
Ordinary people
  Kwamina
The other generation
  Flower drum song
The other half of me
  I had a ball
Other hands, other hearts
  Fanny
The other side of the tracks
  Little me
Our children
  All American
Our language of love
  Irma la douce
Our little secret
  Promises, promises
Out of my dreams
  Oklahoma
Out of the clear blue sky
  Two's company
Over and over
  Make a wish
Over my shoulders
  Evergreen
Over there
  George M!
Pack up your troubles
  Oh, what a lovely war
Panisse and son
  Fanny
Parade
  Camelot
  Candide
A parade in town
  Anyone can whistle
Paris, France
  Make a wish
Paris is Paris again
  Gigi
Paris loves lovers
  Silk stockings
Paris original
  How to succeed in

Processional
   The Sound of music
Public enemy number one
   Anything goes
Push me along in my push
   cart
   George M!
Push the button
   Jamaica
The pussy foot
   Goldilocks
Put on a happy face
   Bye bye Birdie
Put on your Sunday clothes
   Hello, Dolly
A puzzlement
   The King and I
Queen of my heart
   The Three musketeers
Queenie's ballyhoo
   Show boat
A quiet girl
   Wonderful town
Racing with the clock
   Pajama game
Rahadlakum
   Kismet
The rain in Spain
   My fair lady
Raining in my heart
   Dames at sea
The rakish young man with
   the whiskahs
   Bloomer girl
Rat-tat-tat-tat
   Funny girl
Razzle dazzle
   Chicago
The Reader's digest
   A Party
Real live girl
   Little me
The real me
   All American
A red-headed woman
   Porgy and Bess
Remember?

A Little night music
Remember that I care
   Street scene
Restless heart
   Fanny
Reviewing the situation
   Oliver!
Rhymes have I
   Kismet
Ribbons down my back
   Hello, Dolly
The rich
   Carnival
The rich jew and the
   grand inquisitor
   Candide
Ride out the storm
   Seesaw
Ride through the night
   Subways are for sleeping
Ridin' on the moon
   St. Louis woman
The riff song
   The Desert song
Right as the rain
   Bloomer girl
Ring to the name of Rose
   George M!
The Riviera
   The Boy friend
Roll up the ribbons
   I do! I do!
Romance
   The Desert song
A room in Bloomsbury
   The Boy friend
A room with a view
   Cowardy custard
Rosemary
   How to succeed in
      business without
      really trying
Rose's turn
   Gypsy
Rosie
   Bye bye Birdie
Round and round

Stouthearted men
    The New moon
Strange music
    Song of Norway
Stranger in paradise
    Kismet
Stuck with each other
    Tovarich
Student life
    The Student prince
Success
    Cowardy custard
Sue me
    Guys and dolls
Summer nights
    Grease
Summer, summer
    Two gentlemen of Verona
Summertime
    Porgy and Bess
Summertime in Heidelberg
    The Student prince
Summertime love
    Greenwillow
Sun on my face
    Sugar
Sunday
    Flower drum song
Sunday in Cicero Falls
    Bloomer girl
Sunday morning, breakfast
    time
    Jubilee
Sunrise, sunset
    Fiddler on the roof
Sunshine
    Gentlemen prefer blondes
Sunshine girl
    New girl in town
Superstar
    Jesus Christ superstar
Sur la plage
    The Boy friend
Surabaya Johnny
    Berlin to Broadway
        with Kurt Weill
Surprise

Oh captain
    The surrey with the fringe
    on top
    Oklahoma
Sweet and low down
    Tip-toes
Sweet beginning
    The Roar of the
        greasepaint
Sweet Georgia Brown
    Bubbling brown sugar
Sweet Thursday
    Pipe dream
Sweetheart, we need each
    other
    Rio Rita
Swing
    Wonderful town
Swing low, sweet chariot
    Bubbling brown sugar
The sword, the rose,
    and the cape
    Carnival
Take back your mink
    Guys and dolls
Take him
    Pal Joey
Take it slow, Joe
    Jamaica
Take me back to Manhattan
    Anything goes
Taking the moment
    Do I hear a waltz?
Taking a chance on love
    Cabin in the sky
Talking to yourself
    Hallelujah, baby
Tap your troubles away
    Mack & Mabel
Te Deum
    Rex
Tea for two
    No, no, Nanette
The tea party
    Dear world
Telephone girlie
    No, no, Nanette

Annie get your gun
They were you
  The Fantasticks
Things ain't what they used
    to be
  Cabin in the sky
Things to remember
  The Roar of the
    greasepaint
Think
  Pipe dream
Think how it's gonna be
  Applause
Think of something else
  Walking happy
Thinking
  Do I hear a waltz?
This can't be love
  The Boys from Syracuse
This house
  I do! I do!
This is new
  Lady in the dark
This is the life
  Golden boy
This is the life for a man
  Primrose
This Jesus must die
  Jesus Christ superstar
This nearly was mine
  South Pacific
This plum is too ripe
  The Fantasticks
This really isn't me
  First impressions
This time it's true, love
  The Girl who came to
    supper
This time of year
  Finian's rainbow
This was a real nice
    clambake
  Carousel
This week, Americans
  Do I hear a waltz?
This world
  Candide

Those were the good old days
  Damn Yankees
The thought of you
  Fanny
Thoughts will come back to
    me
  The Student prince
Three coins in the fountain
  Words and music
Three paradises
  Oh captain
Throw the anchor away
  By the beautiful sea
Tick-tock
  Company
'Til tomorrow
  Fiorello
Till good luck come my way
  Show boat
Till there was you
  The Music man
Time and again
  Cowardy custard
Time heals everything
  Mack & Mabel
The time of my life
  Salad days
Timid Frieda
  Jacques Brel is alive
    and well and living
    in Paris
Tinkle
  Evergreen
T'morra' t'morra'
  Bloomer girl
To each his Dulcinea
  Man of La Mancha
To life
  Fiddler on the roof
To my wife
  Fanny
Together forever
  I do! I do!
Together wherever we go
  Gypsy
Tokay
  Bitter sweet

House of flowers
Waitin' for my dearie
Brigadoon
Waiting for you
No, no, Nanette
Walking away whistling
Greenwillow
Walking in space
Hair
Wall Street
Dames at sea
Wand'rin' star
Paint your wagon
Wanting you
The New moon
Was I wazir?
Kismet
Was she prettier than I?
High spirits
Wash me in the water
Oh, what a lovely war
Washington Square dance
Call me madam
Wasn't it a simply lovely
wedding?
First impressions
Watch my dust
Hallelujah, baby
Way out west
Babes in arms
The way things are
I can get it for you
wholesale
We both reached for the gun
Chicago
We could be close
Sugar
We kiss in a shadow
The King and I
We make a beautiful pair
Shenandoah
We need a little Christmas
Mame
We open in Venice
Kiss me, Kate
We speak the same language
All American

The wedding
Show boat
The wee golden warrior
Rex
A weekend in the country
A Little night music
Welcome hinges
Bloomer girl
Welcome home
Fanny
Welcome to the theater
Applause
We'll go away together
Street scene
A well known fact
I do! I do!
Wells Fargo wagon
The Music man
We're gonna be all right
Do I hear a waltz?
We're not children
Oh captain
Were thine that special face
Kiss me, Kate
Western people funny
The King and I
We've got it
Seesaw
What a country!
All American
What a nice idea
Two gentlemen of Verona
What a nice municipal park
Jubilee
What a waste
Wonderful town
What are they doing to us
now?
I can get it for you
wholesale
What can you do with a man
The Boys from Syracuse
What did I ever see in him?
Bye bye Birdie
What did I have that I don't
have?
On a clear day you can see

Coco
When you're good to mama
Chicago
When you've got a little
  springtime in your heart
Evergreen
Where are the snows?
I do! I do!
Where can he be?
The Bandwagon
Where can you take a girl?
Promises, promises
Where do I go?
Hair
Where is love?
Oliver!
Where is my son?
Rex
Where is the life that late
  I led?
Kiss me, Kate
Where is the man I married?
High spirits
Where, oh where
Out of this world
Where or when
Babes in arms
Where would you be without
  me?
The Roar of the
  greasepaint
Where's the mate for me?
Show boat
Which way?
All American
While the city sleeps
Golden boy
Whip-poor-will
Sally
White boys
Hair
Whizzin' away along de track
Carmen Jones
Who are you now?
Funny girl
Who can I turn to?
The Roar of the

greasepaint
Who can? You can
The Gay life
Who knows?
I can get it for you
  wholesale
Who knows what might
  have been?
Subways are for
  sleeping
Who taught her everything
Funny girl
Who will buy this wonderful
  morning?
Oliver!
Whoever you are
Promises, promises
A whole lotta sunlight
Raisin
Who'll buy
Lost in the stars
Whoop-ti-ay!
Paint your wagon
Who's got the pain?
Damn Yankees
Who's that girl?
Applause
Why?
Rex
Why be afraid to dance?
Fanny
Why can't the English?
My fair lady
Why can't you behave?
Kiss me, Kate
Why do I love you?
Show boat
Why do the wrong people
  travel?
Cowardy custard
Why go anywhere at all?
The Gay life
Why must the show go on?
Cowardy custard
Why should I wake up?
Cabaret
Wild rose

down
  Sally
You could drive a person
  crazy
  Company
You did it
  My fair lady
You do something to me
  Can-can
You don't know him
  Oh captain
You don't know Paree
  Cole
The you don't want to play
  with me blues
  The Boy friend
You for me
  Saratoga
You gotta have a gimmick
  Gypsy
You have cast your shadow
  on the sea
  The Boys from Syracuse
You have made me love
  Cyrano
You made me love you
  Irene
You mustn't kick it around
  Pal Joey
You say you care
  Gentlemen prefer blondes
You were dead, you know
  Candide
You were there
  Cowardy custard
You will never be lonely
  The Gay life
You wonder how these
  things begin
  The Fantasticks
You'd better love me
  High spirits
You'll never get away from
  me
  Gypsy
You'll never walk alone
  Carousel

Younger generation
  Cowardy custard
Younger than springtime
  South Pacific
Your eyes
  The Three musketeers
You're a grand old flag
  George M!
You're a loveable lunatic
  Seesaw
You're a queer one, Julie
  Jordan
  Carousel
You're always in my arms
  Rio Rita
You're devastating
  Roberta
You're just in love
  Call me madam
You're not alone
  Jacques Brel is alive
    and well and living
    in Paris
You're not the type
  The Gay life
You're so right for me
  Oh captain
You're the top
  Anything goes
You've got to be a little
  crazy
  The Girl in the pink tights
You've got to be carefully
  taught
  South Pacific
You've got what I need
  It's a bird, it's a plane,
    it's Superman
Yum, ticky, ticky, tum, tum
  Carnival
Zigeuner
  Bitter sweet
Zip
  Pal Joey
Zubbediya
  Kismet

★ COMPOSER-LYRICIST INDEX

Evergreen
I married an angel
On your toes
Pal Joey
Rodgers, Richard, and Stephen Sondheim
Do I hear a waltz?
Romberg, Sigmund, and Dorothy Donnelly
The Student prince
Romberg, Sigmund, and Oscar Hammerstein II
The Desert song
The New moon
Schmidt, Harvey, and Tom Jones
Celebration
The Fantasticks
I do! I do!
110 in the shade
Schwartz, Arthur, and Howard Dietz
The Bandwagon
The Gay life
Jennie
Schwartz, Arthur, and Dorothy Fields
By the beautiful sea
A Tree grows in Brooklyn
Strouse, Charles, and Lee Adams
All American
Applause
Bye bye Birdie
Golden boy
It's a bird, it's a plane, it's Superman
Strouse, Charles, and Martin Charnin
Annie
Styne, Jule, and Sammy Cahn
High button shoes
Styne, Jule, and E. Y. Harburg
Darling of the day
Styne, Jule, and Robert Merrill
Funny girl
Sugar
Styne, Jule, and Stephen Sondheim
Gypsy
Van Heusen, James, and Sammy Cahn
Les Poupées de Paris
Skyscraper
Walking happy
Weill, Kurt, and Bertolt Brecht
Happy end
Weill, Kurt, and Langston Hughes

Street scene
Wright, Robert, and George Forrest
   Anya
   Kean
   Kismet
   Song of Norway

★ MAJOR RECORD COMPANY SEQUENTIAL INDEX

Capitol

SO	118	Zorba
SW	198	Celebration
SW	229	Canterbury tales
SO	337	Salvation
S	350	Of thee I sing
T	351	The Desert song; Roberta
ST	408	Wild is love
P	437	The Student prince
S	452	Can-can
S	531	By the beautiful sea
DW	603	Plain and fancy
SO	761	Follies
W	913	Annie get your gun
SWAO	990	The Music man
SWAO	1240	Little Mary Sunshine
SWAO	1321	Fiorello
SWAO	1492	Tenderloin
SWAO	1509	The Unsinkable Molly Brown
SWAO	1560	The Gay life
W	1573	The United States of America
SWAO	1643	Sail away
SWAO	1645	Kwamina
SW	1667	Sail away
SO	1695	No strings

SWAO	1717	A Funny thing happened on the way to the Forum
ST	1784	Oliver
ST	1792	Beyond the fringe
SW	1841	The Student prince
SW	1842	The Desert song
STAO	1940	Tovarich
ST	1941	Our love letter
SW	1966	The New moon
SVAS	2059	Funny girl
SW	2072	Beyond the fringe '64
SW	2073	Cabin in the sky
SVAS	2124	Golden boy
SW	2152	The Unsinkable Molly Brown
SVAS	2191	Ben Franklin in Paris
SVAS	2422	Skyscraper
SVAS	2631	Walking happy
SW	2731	Hello, Solly!
DW	2742	St. Louis woman
T	11649	Flahooley
T	11650	Top banana
T	11651	Of thee I sing
ST	11652	By the beautiful sea
STAO	11653	Tovarich
ST	11654	Beyond the fringe '64
STAO	11655	Golden boy

Columbia OL/OS series

OL	4058	Show boat
OL	4180	South Pacific
OL	4220	Miss Liberty
OL	4290	Gentlemen prefer blondes
OL	4364	Pal Joey
OL	4390	Out of this world
OL	4840	The Pajama game
OL	4850	Kismet
OL	4890	The Girl in pink tights
OL	4963	archy and mehitabel
OL	4969	House of flowers
OL	5090	My fair lady
OL	5118	The Most happy fella
OL	5150	L'il Abner
OL	5240	Simply heaven
OL	5280	Oh captain
OL	5630	Happy end

OL	6770	Blackbirds of 1928
OS	2001	West Side story
OS	2005	Cinderella
OS	2006	Bells are ringing
OS	2007	Goldilocks
OS	2008	Wonderful town
OS	2009	Flower drum song
OS	2013	Juno
OS	2014	First impressions
OS	2015	My fair lady
OS	2017	Gypsy
OS	2018	The Nervous set
KOS	2020	The Sound of music
KOS	2024	A Thurber carnival
KOS	2025	Bye bye Birdie
OS	2026	Christine
OS	2027	Ernest in love
OS	2028	On the town
OS	2029	Irma la douce
OS	2031	Camelot
OS	2040	South Pacific
KOS	2050	The Happiest girl in the world
OS	2060	Kismet
OS	2080	Finian's rainbow
KOS	2120	Kean
KOS	2130	Subways are for sleeping
KOS	2160	All American
KOS	2180	I can get it for you wholesale
KOS	2200	Bravo Giovanni
OS	2210	Pins and needles
OS	2220	Show boat
OS	2250	The Real ambassadors
KOS	2270	Mr. President
OS	2300	Kiss me, Kate
OS	2310	Gentlemen prefer blondes
OS	2320	House of flowers
OS	2330	The Most happy fella
OS	2350	Candide
OS	2360	Annie get your gun
OS	2380	The Student prince
OS	2390	Lady in the dark
KOS	2400	Here's love
KOS	2420	The Girl who came to supper
KOS	2440	What makes Sammy run?
OS	2530	Roberta
OS	2540	Brigadoon
OS	2550	Oh, Kay!

OS	2560	Girl crazy
OS	2570	Babes in arms
OS	2580	The Boys from Syracuse
OS	2590	On your toes
OS	2610	Oklahoma
OS	2630	To Broadway with love
OS	2640	The King and I
KOS	2700	Bajour
OS	2720	The Secret life of Walter Mitty
OS	2730	Cinderella
KOS	2770	Do I hear a waltz?
OS	2810	The Decline and fall of the entire world as seen through the eyes of Cole Porter
KOS	2880	The Zulu and the zayda
KOS	2900	Sweet Charity
OS	2930	The Mad show
KOS	2970	It's a bird, it's a plane, it's Superman
KOS	3000	Mame
KOS	3020	The Apple tree
KOS	3040	Cabaret
KOS	3090	Hallelujah, baby
OS	3100	South Pacific
OS	3130	Now is the time for all good men
KOS	3200	George M!
BOS	3260	Dear world
BOS	3310	1776
OS	3330	Dames at sea
OS	3550	Company

Columbia other series

CL	822	Girl crazy
CL	823	Babes in arms
CL	826	The Student prince
CL	828	Oklahoma
CL	831	The Desert song
CL	837	On your toes
CL	841	Roberta
CL	847	The Boys from Syracuse
CL	1050	Oh, Kay!
CL	1132	Brigadoon
CS	8135	Song of Norway
CS	8568	Kiss me, Kate
CS	8717	Half-past Wednesday
D2S	779	Jacques Brel is alive and well and living in Paris

ELS	354	Anne of Green Gables
JS	35410	Runaways
KS	31456	Jubilee
KS	32265	A Little night music
KS	32266	Irene
KS	32754	Raisin
KS	32961	Over here
ML	4139	Street scene
ML	4405	A Tree grows in Brooklyn
ML	4636	The Desert song
ML	4645	On your toes
ML	4751	The Bandwagon; Anything goes
PC	34032	Me and Bessie
PS	33581	A Chorus line
PS	34197	My fair lady
PS	34712	Annie
PS	35330	On the Twentieth Century
S	30337	The Rothschilds
S	30338	Two by two
S	30563	No, no, Nanette
S	30589	70, girls 70
S	31005	On the town
S	31237	Man of La Mancha
S	32601	The Sound of music
S	32602	Camelot
S	32603	West Side story
S	32604	South Pacific
S	32605	Kismet
S	32606	The Pajama game
S	32607	Gypsy
S	32608	Anyone can whistle
S	32609	Kiss me, Kate
S	32610	Gentlemen prefer blondes
SG	30415	Story theatre
SX	30742	Fiddler on the roof
S2X	32923	Candide

MCA 2000 series

2018	Man of La Mancha
2028	The King and I
2030	Oklahoma
2031	Annie get your gun
2032	Song of Norway
2033	Carousel
2034	Guys and dolls

2035	Porgy and Bess
2050	Wonderful town
2054	Carmen Jones
2055	Call me madam
2071	Lost in the stars
2072	Bloomer girl
2074	The Boy friend
2079	Once upon a mattress

Monmouth-Evergreen 7000 series

7029	Where's Charley?
7036	Lady be good
7037	Funny face
7043	Nymph errant; Oh, Kay!
7049	Anything goes; Evergreen; On your toes
7050	The Three musketeers; The Vagabond king
7051	The New moon
7052	Tip-toes; Wildflower
7053	Sally
7054	The Desert song; The Student prince
7057	Irene
7058	Rio Rita; Show boat
7071	Primrose
7073	Call me madam; Can-can

RCA LOC/LSO 1000 series

1000	The Desert song
1001	Brigadoon
1006	Paint your wagon
1007	Wish you were here
1008	New faces of 1952
1010	Hazel Flagg
1011	Show biz
1014	The Golden apple
1015	Fanny
1016	Silk stockings
1018	The Boy friend
1019	Peter Pan
1021	Damn Yankees
1027	New girl in town
1036	Jamaica
1045	Say, darling
1048	Redhead
1049	Darling of the day
1050	Take me along
1051	Saratoga
1057	Finian's rainbow
1060	Wildcat
1064	Let it ride

1065	Milk and honey
1066	How to succeed in business without really trying
1078	Little me
1083	Jennie
1085	110 in the shade
1087	Hello, Dolly
1090	Les Poupées de Paris
1092	The King and I
1093	Fiddler on the roof
1097	Pipe dream
1098	Me and Juliet
1099	Allegro
1102	Silk stockings
1103	Jamaica
1104	Redhead
1105	Do-re-mi
1106	New girl in town
1107	High button shoes
1108	Wish you were here
1109	The Roar of the greasepaint
1110	Half a sixpence
1111	Flora, the red menace
1112	Kismet
1114	Carousel
1124	Annie get your gun
1126	Show boat
1128	I do! I do!
1137	By Jupiter
1140	Cricket on the hearth
1142	How now Dow Jones
1143	Hair
1144	The Happy time
1147	Hello, Dolly
1148	Your own thing
1149	Darling of the day
1150	Hair
1151	The Believers
1153	How to steal an election
1161	Promenade
1162	Jimmy
1163	DsinHAIRited
1166	Joy
1169	The Last sweet days of Isaac
1171	Inner city

RCA other series

ABL	1-0404	Gigi
ABL	1-1683	Rex
ABL	1-2360	Starting here, starting now
ABL	1-2760	Flora, the red menace
ANL	1-0986	Hair
ANL	1-2849	Hello, Dolly
ARL	1-1011	Goodtime Charley
ARL	1-1019	Shenandoah
ARL	1-1367	Pacific overtures
AVM	1-1741	Show boat
CBL	2-1851	Side by side by Sondheim
CBL	2-2965	Ain't misbehavin'
CBM	1-2032	Call me madam
CBM	1-2033	Make a wish
CBM	1-2034	Seventeen
CBM	1-2206	New faces of 1952
CBM	1-2207	Hazel Flagg
CBM	1-2208	Silk stockings
CBM	1-2757	Two's company
CBM	1-2758	Allegro
CPL	2-0419	The Carpenter's son
CRL	2-5054	Cole
LBL	1-5004	Gypsy
LM	1882	Lady in the dark
LM	2008	Show boat
LOP	1001	Rose Marie
LPM	1048	Carousel
LPM	1984	Kiss me, Kate
LPV	503	Lady in the dark
LRL	1-5079	Words and music
LRL	1-5090	A Little night music
LSC	2339	The Student prince
LSC	2440	The Desert song
LSC	2509	The Vagabond king
LSO	2001	Greenwillow
LSO	6010	Cowardy custard
LSOD	2002	Do-re-mi
LSOD	2004	Oliver
LSOD	2006	On a clear day you can see forever
LSOD	2007	Hello, Dolly
LSOD	2009	Maggie Flynn
LSP	2274	My fair lady; Paint your wagon
LSP	2275	Gigi
LSP	4115	What it was, was love
LSP	4719	Oh say can you see?

★ APPENDIX

The following records appear to have been released, but full
information was not available:

All in love.   OC   Mercury 2204/6204 (1962)

Billy Barnes L. A.   OC Criterion 1001/S1001 (1963)

Billy Barnes revue.   OC Decca 9076/79076 (1959)

Bye bye Birdie.   OC (London)   Mercury 13000/17000 (1964)

Cindy.   OC   ABC   OC/SOC   2 (1964)

Clown around.   OC   RCA LSO   1174 (1972)

Committee.   OC   Reprise 2023/S2023 (1964)

Cry for us all.   OC   Project 3   TS 1000 (1970)

Different times.   OC   RCA LSO   1173 (1972)

Dr. Selavy's magic theatre.   OC   United Artists LA 275-G
   (1974)

Family affair.   OC   United Artists 4099/5099 (1962)

First reader.   OC   Polydor 247 002 (1970)

Fly blackbird.   OC Mercury   2206/6206 (1962)

Four below strikes back.   OC   Offbeat 4017 (1960)

Good evening.   OC   Island 9298 (1974)
   Features Peter Cook and Dudley Moore.

Grass harp.   OC   Painted Smiles 1354 (1972)
   Music by Claibe Richardson;   book and lyrics by Kenward
   Elmslie;   based on the novel by Truman Capote.

The Great waltz.   OC   Capitol SVAS 2426 (1965)

Greenwich Village, U.S.A.   OC   20th Century Fox 4005/S4005
   (1960)

Hair.   OC (London)   Atco S-7002 (1969)

Henry, sweet Henry.   OC   ABC OC/SOC 4 (1968)
   Features Don Ameche.   Music and lyrics by Robert
   Merrill;   book by Nunnally Johnson;   based on The world
   of Henry Orient, by Nora Johnson.

House of flowers.   OC(1968)   United Artists 5180 (1968)

Illya darling.   OC   United Artists 8901/9901 (1967)

King Kong.   OC(London)   London 5762 (1963)

Lilac time.   Angel   35817/S35817 (1960)

Lively set.   OC   Decca 9119/79119 (1964)

Lock up your daughters.   OC   London 5766 (1963)

Man from the east.   OC   Island SMAS 9334 (1974)

Man with a load of mischief.   OC   Kapp 5508 (1967)

Minnie's boys.   OC   Project 3 TS 6002 (1970)

Oh!   Calcutta!   OC   Aidart 9903 (1969)

Oh, Kay!   OC   20th Century Fox 4003/S4003 (1960)

Oliver. OC(London) London Decca SPA 30 (1974)

On the brighter side. OC London 5767 (1964)

On the flip side. OC Decca 4836/74836 (1967)

One over the eight. OC London 5760 (1963)
    Features Vera Zorina, Bobby Van, and Elaine Stritch.

One touch of Venus. OC Decca 9122/79122 (1965)
    Features Mary Martin and Kenny Baker. Music by
    Kurt Weill; lyrics by Ira Gershwin and Ogden Nash.

Pieces of eight. OC Offbeat 4016 (1959)

Pieces of eight. OC London 5761 (1963)

The Prince and the pauper. OC London 28001/98001 (1964)

Riverwind. OC London 48001/78001 (1963)

Rocky horror show. OC Ode 77026 (1974)

Salad days. OC London 5765 (1963)

Shoestring '57. OC Offbeat 4012 (1957)

Shoestring revue. OC Offbeat 4011 (1956)

Show girl. Roulette 80001/S80001 (1962)
    Features Carol Channing and Jules Munshin. Music by
    George Gershwin; lyrics by Ira Gershwin and Gus Kahn;
    book by William Anthony McGuire and J. P. McEvoy.

Take five. OC Offbeat 4013 (1958)

Tom Jones. OC Theatre Productions 5900/9000 (1964)

Tom Sawyer. OC Decca 8432 (1957)

Touch. OC Ampex 50102 (1972)